Ember.js Web Development with Ember CLI

Build ambitious single-page web applications using the power of Ember.js and Ember CLI

Suchit Puri

PUBLISHING

BIRMINGHAM - MUMBAI

Ember.js Web Development with Ember CLI

First published: May 2015

Production reference: 1220515

Published by Packt Publishing Ltd.
Livery Place
35 Livery Street
Birmingham B3 2PB, UK.

ISBN 978-1-78439-584-1

www.packtpub.com

Credits

Author
Suchit Puri

Reviewers
Michał Karzyński
David Sevcik

Commissioning Editor
Edward Bowkett

Acquisition Editor
Harshit D Jhaveri

Content Development Editors
Neetu Ann Mathew
Rohit Kumar Singh

Technical Editor
Ruchi Desai

Copy Editors
Sonia Michelle Cheema
Khushnum Mistry
Sameen Siddiqui

Project Coordinator
Mary Alex

Proofreaders
Stephen Copestake
Safis Editing

Indexer
Monica Ajmera Mehta

Graphics
Sheetal Aute
Jason Monteiro

Production Coordinator
Arvindkumar Gupta

Cover Work
Arvindkumar Gupta

About the Author

Suchit Puri is a full-stack software developer and holds a master's degree in software systems.

He has held senior development and technical management positions at some of the world's most prominent companies, such as Huawei, Progress Software, and ThoughtWorks. He is currently working for a Delhi-based start-up called Wingify, which is growing rapidly. He specializes in project inceptions, analysis, coding, deployments, and automation, and clients ranging from small, fast-paced start-ups to big multinationals have benefited from his expertise.

He is also a sought-after speaker and has given presentations at various technical conferences, including JSConf 2014, held in Bangalore, where he spoke about his experience with Ember.js.

Suchit was introduced to Ember.js during its pre-beta days and has been leading a team of developers to create applications for different clients, including one of the largest property evaluators in Australia.

He has been a contributor to books such as *Talking With Tech Leads* by Patrik Kua.

Suchit's blog can be found at `http://suchitpuri.com/`.

Acknowledgments

I would like to thank my parents (Brij and Seema) and my sister, Charvi. This endeavor has been possible due to your guidance and encouragement. Thanks for believing in me.

I'd like to give special thanks my wife, Aastha, for her overwhelming support and encouragement throughout the course of writing this book. Thank you for being patient with me on countless weekends and late nights when I have been writing.

I would also like to thank all the editors of Packt Publishing, who have been really helpful, especially Harshit Jhaveri, for being a patient and professional mentor.

Last but not least, I would like to dedicate my book to my grandfather, the late Mr. Krishan Lal Vij. He has always been an inspiration in my life.

Gyanshakti-samaroodhah tattwamala vibhooshitah.

Bhukti-mukti-pradata cha tasmai Shri Gurave Namah.

My salutations to that glorious Gurudev, who is established in knowledge and power, is adorned with the garland of knowledge, and who grants both worldly prosperity and spiritual liberation.

About the Reviewers

Michał Karzyński has a scientific research background in the areas of molecular biology and bioinformatics. He is currently working as a systems architect, full-stack web developer, and a consultant, specializing in dynamic languages, particularly, JavaScript and Python.

Michał loves designing and implementing large, ambitious, and scalable web applications. Over the years, he has gained experience in and an expert knowledge of numerous MVC frameworks in JavaScript, such as Ember.js, AngularJS, and ExtJS, and Django, Rails, Flask, Express, and CodeIgniter on the server.

He also loves Linux and is an expert in server administration and Cloud computing. Last year, he wrote a book on server administration called *Webmin Administrator's Cookbook, Packt Publishing*. As a consultant, Michał was responsible for designing and deploying the Cloud infrastructure for a number of companies in Silicon Valley and around the world.

Michał is currently employed as a software engineer at Intel. He also runs the consulting company Atarnia.com. He writes a blog, which can be found at `http://michal.karzynski.pl`.

David Sevcik is a full-stack developer with many years of experience with Ruby and JavaScript on both frontend and backend. He applies his knowledge for projects in various industries, such as project management and automotive and customer research for companies based in the UK and the Czech Republic. He is an active member of open source communities and has contributed to several Ember projects.

www.PacktPub.com

Support files, eBooks, discount offers, and more

For support files and downloads related to your book, please visit www.PacktPub.com.

Did you know that Packt offers eBook versions of every book published, with PDF and ePub files available? You can upgrade to the eBook version at www.PacktPub.com and as a print book customer, you are entitled to a discount on the eBook copy. Get in touch with us at service@packtpub.com for more details.

At www.PacktPub.com, you can also read a collection of free technical articles, sign up for a range of free newsletters and receive exclusive discounts and offers on Packt books and eBooks.

https://www2.packtpub.com/books/subscription/packtlib

Do you need instant solutions to your IT questions? PacktLib is Packt's online digital book library. Here, you can search, access, and read Packt's entire library of books.

Why subscribe?

- Fully searchable across every book published by Packt
- Copy and paste, print, and bookmark content
- On demand and accessible via a web browser

Free access for Packt account holders

If you have an account with Packt at www.PacktPub.com, you can use this to access PacktLib today and view 9 entirely free books. Simply use your login credentials for immediate access.

Table of Contents

Preface

Ember.js Web Development with Ember CLI is a must read for the next generation of web developers who will enjoy building powerful single-page web applications using the simplicity of Ember CLI and sophistication of the upcoming Ember 2.0. It is expected to be the lightest, thinnest, and most powerful version of Ember.js ever, with stability and backward compatibility important parts of its roadmap. This also means that many of the features of Ember.js 2.0 are already available today. This book will put you in a pole position to leverage them and stay ahead of the pack.

Unlike many other books that merely skim the surface, this book has a strong focus on Ember CLI, which will soon be the de-facto mode to build apps with Ember.js. It is a complete guide to creating powerful, scalable, and maintainable single-page web applications using Ember.js with Ember CLI.

What this book covers

Chapter 1, Getting Started with Building Ambitious Ember.js Applications with Ember CLI, will get you started with your first Ember.js application using Ember CLI and you will learn about its MVC pattern.

Chapter 2, Understanding Ember.js Object-oriented Patterns, covers the object-oriented design principles used in Ember.js, including classes and objects.

Chapter 3, Rendering Using Templates, shows you how to use the templating system of Ember.js and its default helpers.

Chapter 4, Managing Application State Using Ember.js Routes, explains how to manage the state of your application using Ember.Router.

Chapter 5, Handling Display Logic Using Ember.js Controllers, covers how to use controllers to communicate display logic to templates.

Chapter 6, Communicating with the API Server Using ember-data, shows you how to communicate with your backend server using ember-data models.

Chapter 7, Building Reusable Components, explains building reusable Ember.js components and learning how to customize them.

What you need for this book

You need a latest browser to run the code samples mentioned in the book. To access the code from GitHub, you will need to install Git version control, optionally, the code samples can be downloaded as a ZIP file from the links mentioned in the following *Downloading the example code* section.

Ember CLI runs on Node.js and hence, it is important to install the latest version of Node.js. Bower is used to manage the dependencies of your Ember CLI application. The instructions to install Git, Node.js, and bower can be found in the *Setting up your first Ember.js application using Ember CLI* section of the first chapter.

Who this book is for

This book targets JavaScript developers who are starting out, as well as developers who have prior Ember.js experience and want to transition their application to the latest Ember.js version with Ember CLI.

Conventions

In this book, you will find a number of text styles that distinguish between different kinds of information. Here are some examples of these styles and an explanation of their meaning.

Code words in text, database table names, folder names, filenames, file extensions, pathnames, dummy URLs, user input, and Twitter handles are shown as follows: "If you look inside `environment.js`, you will notice that the environment module exports the configurations in an ENV object."

A block of code is set as follows:

```
var base = Ember.Object.extend({
  baseProperty: true
});
var derived = base.extend({
  derivedProperty:false
```

```
});
var derivedObject = derived.create();
console.log(derivedObject.get('baseProperty'));
console.log(derivedObject.get('derivedProperty'));
```

When we wish to draw your attention to a particular part of a code block, the relevant lines or items are set in bold:

```
redirect: function(){
  this.transitionTo("commits.index");
}
```

Any command-line input or output is written as follows:

```
ember new my-first-ember-app
```

New terms and **important words** are shown in bold. Words that you see on the screen, for example, in menus or dialog boxes, appear in the text like this: "The contents of the template should have a **Show More** and **Show Less** button."

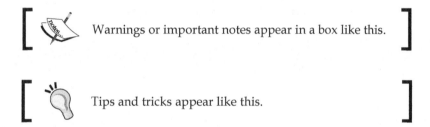

Warnings or important notes appear in a box like this.

Tips and tricks appear like this.

Reader feedback

Feedback from our readers is always welcome. Let us know what you think about this book—what you liked or disliked. Reader feedback is important for us as it helps us develop titles that you will really get the most out of.

To send us general feedback, simply e-mail feedback@packtpub.com, and mention the book's title in the subject of your message.

If there is a topic that you have expertise in and you are interested in either writing or contributing to a book, see our author guide at www.packtpub.com/authors.

Customer support

Now that you are the proud owner of a Packt book, we have a number of things to help you to get the most from your purchase.

Downloading the example code

You can download the example code files from your account at http://www.packtpub.com for all the Packt Publishing books you have purchased. If you purchased this book elsewhere, you can visit http://www.packtpub.com/support and register to have the files e-mailed directly to you. Optionally, the code samples can also be downloaded from https://github.com/suchitpuri/emberjs-essentials.

Errata

Although we have taken every care to ensure the accuracy of our content, mistakes do happen. If you find a mistake in one of our books—maybe a mistake in the text or the code—we would be grateful if you could report this to us. By doing so, you can save other readers from frustration and help us improve subsequent versions of this book. If you find any errata, please report them by visiting http://www.packtpub.com/submit-errata, selecting your book, clicking on the **Errata Submission Form** link, and entering the details of your errata. Once your errata are verified, your submission will be accepted and the errata will be uploaded to our website or added to any list of existing errata under the Errata section of that title.

To view the previously submitted errata, go to https://www.packtpub.com/books/content/support and enter the name of the book in the search field. The required information will appear under the **Errata** section.

Piracy

Piracy of copyrighted material on the Internet is an ongoing problem across all media. At Packt, we take the protection of our copyright and licenses very seriously. If you come across any illegal copies of our works in any form on the Internet, please provide us with the location address or website name immediately so that we can pursue a remedy.

Please contact us at copyright@packtpub.com with a link to the suspected pirated material.

We appreciate your help in protecting our authors and our ability to bring you valuable content.

Questions

If you have a problem with any aspect of this book, you can contact us at questions@packtpub.com, and we will do our best to address the problem.

1
Getting Started with Building Ambitious Ember.js Applications with Ember CLI

In this chapter, we will briefly discuss the history of ambitious web applications. We will be introducing the Ember.js MVC framework, followed by a detailed guide to setting up your first Ember.js application.

This chapter covers:

- The evolution of ambitious web applications
- An introduction to Ember.js
- The Ember.js MVC pattern
- An introduction to Ember CLI:
    - Asset pipeline
    - Modules
    - Managing dependencies of your application
    - Content security add-on

- Setting up your first Ember.js application:
    - Prerequisites
    - Creating a new application
    - The app folder structure

     °   Supporting files and folders

     °   Running your first Ember.js application

- Building and deploying your Ember CLI application

- Migrating existing Ember applications to Ember CLI

- Code samples used in this book

The evolution of ambitious web applications

Ambitious web applications have had different meanings at different times in the past. With the evolution of Internet applications and frameworks, today's ambitious web applications are getting closer and closer to desktop applications, giving really immersive user experience.

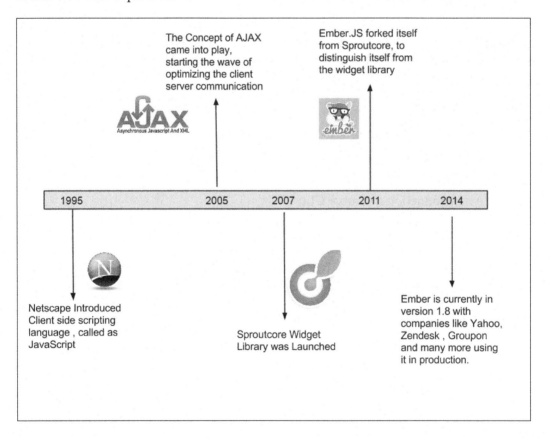

Web applications started with a simple client server model wherein the server used to send all the static content written in HTML markup language to the browser. The browser used to render the content on the client side to display the necessary information. It was possible to collect user data using `<form>` tags that submitted the input field details to the server, which responded with the complete HTML.

In 1995, Netscape introduced a client side scripting language called **JavaScript**. It was intended to run inside a browser to handle things such as form validations, thus giving users an interactive experience. Following that, Java by Sun Microsystems introduced the concept of web applications in 1999 with their "Servlet" specification, thereby enabling a big community of Java developers to write web applications.

10 years later, in 2005, the term **AJAX (asynchronous JavaScript and XML)** started to come into play wherein, instead of sending and receiving the entire HTML content from the server, the client could ask for specific information from the server. This was one of the first steps taken to optimize browser-server communication. This also greatly improved the user experience, as the user, instead of going to multiple pages, got everything on one page.

In 2007, a JavaScript library called SproutCore was launched. The library became popular when Apple announced in 2008 that its MobileMe application was using the framework. In December 2011, the SproutCore 2 framework was renamed Ember.js to distinguish itself from SproutCore 1.x, which was a widget-centric library. Thus, Ember.js introduced the **MVC (Model View Controller)** design pattern to build modern single page web applications.

An introduction to Ember.js

Ember.js is a JavaScript framework based on the MVC design pattern. It tries to bring proven design principles and practices into modern web-based application development and lets you focus on solving core business problems.

Ember.js is a highly opinionated framework and takes a lot of inspiration from the Ruby on Rails convention over configuration philosophy. **Convention over configuration**, also known as **coding by convention**, is a design philosophy wherein things work as expected, provided they follow a common set of guidelines.

One example of convention over configuration in the MVC world would be, if there was a class called HomeController, the framework would automatically look for a model class named Home, and make the instance of the model available to the HomeController class. The benefit we get from this is that we did not wire up the controller and model in any configuration file. If we follow the naming guidelines set up by the framework, it takes care of injecting the correct model class to the controller. This results in code that is more concise and follows a particular standard of doing things.

Ember.js is full of such convention over configuration methods, and we shall discuss them later in the chapter.

The Ember.js MVC pattern

The MVC design pattern has been around for a long time now. It provides a good way of segregating your application into well-defined interacting components. Traditionally, the MVC pattern was mostly used to build server-side applications. But many JavaScript frameworks are now trying to use this pattern to build better client-side rich web applications. Ember.js tries to bring in a variation of the MVC pattern to build robust JavaScript-heavy single page web applications.

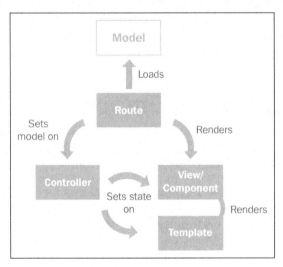

Ember.js MVC Design Pattern

Let's look at how Ember.js tries to design its MVC pattern. As you can see in the preceding image, there are five main components of its MVC pattern.

- **Router/Route** is the entry point of the application. It manages the state of the application by monitoring the change in URL patterns and then injects/instantiates **Controller** and **Model** objects.

- The **Controller** is used to manage the transient state of the application, a state that is not persisted to the server. Often you would want to change or decorate the properties received as part of the model object, to present it in a better way to your users. Such properties and transformation logic should go in controllers.

- **Model** classes encapsulate the data on which controllers and views work. The Model can be a simple JavaScript object or an `ember-data` model object.

- **View/Component** classes encapsulate templates and enable you to make custom reusable elements.

- **Templates** or handlebar templates enable you to divide your application into reusable HTML components. **Handlebar** templates are a mix of HTML markup and custom markup that lets you effortlessly bind the data present in controllers and models with the view.

As you can see from the above description of the layers, Ember.js has very well defined roles and responsibilities for every component. Ember.js attempts to solve the most common and tedious problem you experience while building a single page web application, by providing all the necessary boilerplate code and components. It lets you focus on building beautiful single page web applications, rather than managing the code to wire up things together. This leads to applications that are well designed, extensible, and easy to understand.

An introduction to Ember CLI

JavaScript as a language has come a long way from providing simple dynamic validations, to building complex single page web application. With this evolution, the problems you encounter while building a complex web application also surface in the JavaScript world. These include some of the following:

- Managing deployments
- Linting
- API stubbing for development
- Accessing APIs via proxy

- Running tests
- Continuous integration
- Managing the dependencies of your application

Until now, developers working on ambitious web applications have been trying to solve these issues using different independent sets of tools. Integrating your framework with these tools can take some time and effort. What if there was a tool that could manage all of these and more, irrespective of the server or language you are integrating your single page web applications with?

Ember CLI aims to be one such Ember.js command line utility that you can use to build, develop, and ship ambitious single page web applications.

Ember CLI was based on the Ember App Kit project, which is now deprecated.

Asset pipeline

Ember CLI includes the fast asset pipeline **broccoli** (can be found at `https://github.com/broccolijs/broccoli`). Broccoli draws heavy inspiration from the Rails asset pipeline. It runs on node.js and is independent of the backend platform you are working with.

One of the most common ways to handle asset compilation and minifying is to use the Grunt task runner, or a similar tool. Let's say you are working on an application that involves the compilation of CoffeeScript, Sass, and other similar assets. Now to make these assets available to our application, you will have to write a Grunt task that does the compilation.

When you start the active development of your application, you will realize that running the Grunt task after making any changes to your CoffeeScript or Sass files is cumbersome and time-consuming. So, you start using `grunt watch` in your application to rebuild your entire application whenever you make any changes anywhere in your application. But very soon, when your application grows in size and complexity, you will realize that `grunt watch` is taking too much time as you are rebuilding your entire application, even if only one of the Sass files has been changed.

Broccoli, on the other hand, figures out which files have changed and only rebuilds those that were modified. This means that rebuilding is now a constant time with the number of files in your application, as you generally only rebuild one file.

This is just one example of what broccoli is capable of. It has many more useful optimizations to make your development and build process simple and fast.

Some of the assets that are supported by Broccoli include:

- Handlebars
- Emblem
- LESS
- Sass
- Compass
- Stylus
- CoffeeScript
- EmberScript
- Minified JS and CSS

Every Ember CLI project will contain a file called `Brocfile.js` present at the root of the project. This is the definition file and contains build-specific instructions for your project.

Modules

Before Ember CLI or the Ember App kit, Ember applications used to define their component in the global namespace. The name of these components was very important, as the Ember resolver used to find these components in the global namespace using their name.

Using global namespaces for your application is manageable for smaller applications, but it is definitely not a recommended way of developing your application, as it exposes all the components of the application, and allows you to manually start including components in other components that should not be accessible there.

Ember CLI tries to address these concerns by including the ES6 module transpiler (can be found at `https://github.com/esnext/es6-module-transpiler`). The ES6 module transpiler lets you write a subset of ES6 or the EcmaScript6 module syntax, and then compiles it to the **AMD (asynchronous module definition)** that is supported by RequireJS (`http://requirejs.org/`).

Using modules will enable you to define and export your class definitions, and lets you import them wherever required. It does not expose all of the app components to the rest of the application and hence, is more modular and abstraction friendly.

Ember CLI also comes with its own resolver that understands the application structure, and uses the file names as the convention to make the required modules available to other dependent modules. For example, your route in `routes/product.js` will know to use the controller in `controllers/product.js`, and the template in `templates/product.hbs`.

Prior to Ember CLI, the default resolver used to work by resolving the names from the global namespace. Something similar to the following:

```
App.IndexRoute = Ember.Route.extend({
  model: function() {
    return ['something','else'];
  }
});
```

This would resolve to index route of the application that is defined `App`. But with the new resolver (found at `https://github.com/ember-cli/ember-resolver`), you don't need to write or pollute the global namespace of your application, as it works on ES6 semantics.

The above index route will now be picked up from the `app/routes/index.js` file, which should return a valid ES6 module definition.

This is how a sample ES6 module-compatible index route will look:

```
// app/routes/index.js
import Ember from 'ember'
export default Ember.Route.extend({
  model: function(){
    return ["something","else"];
  }
});
```

Ember CLI's new resolver works by looking for the ES6 modules exported from corresponding files.

You can see that the names of the components are now picked up from designated file locations. The resolver looks for the module that is exported from `app/routes/index.js`, and initializes the index route of the application with the same. The same also applies to rest of the components in the Ember.js framework, including views, controllers, components, adapters, and models.

Managing the dependencies of your application

Ember CLI uses **bower** (`http://bower.io/`) as the default tool to manage the dependencies of your application. Bower lets you easily manage and keep your frontend dependencies up-to-date. Bower works by looking for and installing the dependent packages that you defined in its definition file.

Ember CLI also uses **npm** or the **node package manager** (`https://www.npmjs.com/`) to manage its internal dependencies. The best part about the above dependency management tools is that they are already integrated with the rest of the components, including the asset pipeline, and work flawlessly with Ember.js applications.

Content security add-on

Ember CLI comes with the content security add-on, which activates the content security policy on modern browsers while running the development server. This plugin, when enabled, sets the `Content-Security-Policy` HTTP header to the response that is sent from the Ember CLI development server. This guards your application against XSS attacks.

The default behavior for this plugin is to allow content form 'self'. This means that by default, you will only be allowed to load in assets from the domain that is serving the application. In order to change the content security settings of your development Ember CLI express server, you can change the settings in the `config/environment.js` file present in your project directory.

The `Content-Security-Policy` is currently supported by Chrome (25+), Safari (7+), and Firefox (23+).

Setting up your first Ember.js application using Ember CLI

Now that we have some understanding of the features provided by Ember CLI, let's jump into how to set up your Ember CLI project.

Prerequisites

Before you set up your Ember CLI, you need to satisfy the dependencies required by the project.

- **Node** – Ember CLI runs on node.js and hence it is important to install the latest version of node. To do that, please follow the instructions mentioned at `http://nodejs.org`.

- **Ember CLI** – Once you have successfully installed node on your machine, it's time to install the `ember-cli` package using node package manager by running:

  ```
  npm install -g ember-cli
  ```

  This will install the Ember command line utility in your environment. Once the npm command finishes successfully, run `ember help` to check if the `ember` command line was installed properly.

- **Git** – Please make sure that Git (`http://git-scm.com/book/en/v2/Getting-Started-Installing-Git`) is installed before installing bower, as some bower packages require it to be fetched and installed.

- **Bower** – Ember CLI integrates with bower so that you can manage the frontend dependencies effectively in your project. To install bower, run the following program:

  ```
  npm install -g bower
  ```

  Similar to `ember-cli`, bower (`http://bower.io/`) will give you access to the `bower` command in your terminal.

  To check if bower was installed properly, run `bower -help` in your terminal to see if you get the proper help message.

- **PhantomJS** – Ember CLI uses PhantomJS (`http://phantomjs.org/`) to run your integration test. PhantomJS is a WebKit environment that can open your web applications in headless mode. It also provides a JavaScript API that gives you the capability to programmatically navigate, take screenshots, assert on page content, and more. To install PhantonJS, run:

  ```
  npm install -g phantomjs
  ```

Creating a new application

Now that all your dependencies for Ember CLI are installed, let's create a new project using the Ember command line tool installed.

Run the following command in the terminal at the location where you want to create a new project:

```
ember new my-first-ember-app
```

Once the above command finishes, it will create a new application inside the my-first-ember-app folder. It will also generate the complete application structure for you, with all the dependencies for your application already installed.

Let's see what's generated inside the my-first-ember-app folder.

The app folder structure

The app folder structure is shown in the following screenshot:

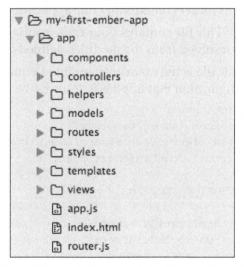

The contents of the app folder generated within my-first-ember-app

Let's look at the app folder first. The app folder contains your Ember.js application building blocks:

- app/components/ – This folder should contain all the components of your application. According to Ember CLI resolver conventions, the components' names should have a - in them. In the latest versions of Ember, there has been a lot more focus on components, rather than views. We will discuss more about components in *Chapter 7, Building Reusable Components*.

- `app/controllers/` – This folder should contain the controller modules of your application. Controllers are covered in *Chapter 5, Handling Display Logic Using Ember.js Controllers.*

- `app/helpers/` – This should contain all the handlebars helpers of your application. Handlebars and helper methods are covered in *Chapter 3, Rendering Using Templates.*

- `app/models/` – This contains all the `ember-data` model modules. You can learn more about `ember-data` and model classes in *Chapter 6, Communicating with the API Server Using ember-data.*

- `app/routes/` – All application routes should go inside this folder. Child routes are defined inside `app/routes/parent/child.js`. Routing is covered in *Chapter 4, Managing Application State Using Ember.js Routes.*

- `app/styles/` – This folder should contain all your style sheets.

- `app/templates/` – This folder should have all the `handlebars/HTMLBars` templates. You can learn more about templates in *Chapter 3, Rendering Using Templates.*

- `app/views/` – This folder contains all your application views.

- `app/router.js` – This file contains your route configuration. The routes defined here are resolved from the modules defined in `app/routes/`.

- `app/app.js` – This file is the main entry point of your application and contains the configuration that applies to your Ember.js application.

```
import Ember from 'ember';
import Resolver from 'ember/resolver';
import loadInitializers from 'ember/load-initializers';
import config from './config/environment';

Ember.MODEL_FACTORY_INJECTIONS = true;

var App = Ember.Application.extend({
  modulePrefix: config.modulePrefix,
  podModulePrefix: config.podModulePrefix,
  Resolver: Resolver
});

loadInitializers(App, config.modulePrefix);

export default App;
```

This is what the default generated `app.js` looks like. As you can see, it exports your Ember.js application, which inherits the `Ember.Application` class.

- `app/index.html` – This is the main file for your single page web application. This is where the structure of your application is laid out. It includes the JavaScript and CSS files of your application. This file also includes certain hooks for the Ember CLI add-ons using `{{content-for 'head'}}`, `{{content-for 'head-footer'}}`, `{{content-for 'body-footer'}}`, and other such tags. These tags should not be touched unless you are developing your own add-on.

Supporting files and folders

Let's look at the rest of the generated files and folders present in `my-first-ember-app` directory.

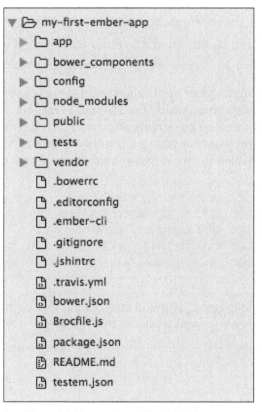

The complete files and folders generated by the Ember command line tool

As you can see, there are a lot of folders and files generated to help you start working on your project faster than ever.

- bower_components – This folder contains all the dependencies which the Ember CLI installs via bower. The bower components are listed in its configuration file bower.json present at the same level.

- config/environment.js – The config folder is the placeholder for your application configurations. Ember CLI supports different configurations for different environments. By default, it has already created configurations for your application for development, test, and production environments. You can also add your configuration for any other custom environment you wish to use for your application.

If you look inside environment.js, you will notice that the environment module exports the configurations in an ENV object.

The ENV object can be imported into other files using the following statement:

```
import ENV from my-first-ember-app/config/environment';
```

To enable logging for your application in the development environment, you can add the configuration inside the if (environment === 'development') section. It is commented by default, so you can just uncomment the configuration you want for your environment. Here is how the final code block with logging enabled for the development environment will look:

```
if (environment === 'development') {
    ENV.APP.LOG_RESOLVER = true;
    ENV.APP.LOG_ACTIVE_GENERATION = true;
    ENV.APP.LOG_TRANSITIONS = true;
    ENV.APP.LOG_TRANSITIONS_INTERNAL = true;
    ENV.APP.LOG_VIEW_LOOKUPS = true;
}
```

Once you enable logging, you will start seeing the log messages inside the console of the development tools of your browser:

Log messages being logged in the code of your browser's development tools

By default, Ember.js will be attached to the body of your HTML document. You can change that by setting the ENV.APP.rootElement = '#ember-cli' property in the environment.js.

This will attach your Ember application to the DOM element that has an ID ember-cli. This is useful for cases where you are building a component of an existing website using Ember.js, and want to attach your div to an existing element.

- node_modules – This folder contains the node dependencies used by Ember CLI.

- public – This folder contains assets that should be copied as they are to the root of the packaged application, these assets will not go through the broccoli asset pipeline used by Ember CLI.

- vendor – This folder should contain libraries which cannot be installed using bower or npm. The libraries in vendor should then be imported into the broccoli asset pipeline, by adding the necessary import statements in Brocfile.js.

- test – This folder contains helpers and resolvers to run unit and integration tests using the Ember testing module for our application.

To run tests for your application, just run:

```
ember test
```

At your project's root location, it will run the unit and integration test in headless mode using phantomJS.

In order to continually run tests whenever you change any file, just run the following command:

```
ember test -server
```

You can also run tests in the browser when running the development server by navigating to http://localhost:4200/test/.

Ember CLI uses Qunit as its testing library, though you can plug in other libraries using their Ember add-ons.

- Brocfile.js – This file contains the build instructions for the broccoli asset pipeline. If you add additional libraries such as bootstrap, you will have to include the assets of these libraries in Brocfile.js in order for them to be processed by the asset pipeline.

```
app.import('bower_components/bootstrap/dist/css/
  bootstrap.css');
```

This will tell the asset pipeline to include `bootstrap.css` in your application.

```
app.import('vendor/my_library/mylibrary.js');
```

This will tell the asset pipeline to include `mylibrary.js` present in the `vendor` directory.

- `bower.json` – This file is the configuration file for bower, and contains the dependencies of your application that need to be installed via bower.
- `package.json` – This is the node package manager configuration file. It contains the node.js dependencies required by your application.

Running your first Ember.js application

Now since we have understood all the libraries and the structure of our first Ember.js application.

To run your Ember CLI application while developing, run the following command in the projects root directory:

```
ember server
```

This will start a development server at port 4200. To run your application on a different port, you can pass in the port configuration to the Ember CLI as follows:

```
ember server -port 4300
```

Or you can add the following configuration to the `.ember-cli` file present in your project's root directory to permanently change the default configuration:

```
{
  "port": 4300
}
```

Building and deploying your Ember CLI application

In order to build your application to be deployed in the production environment, you will have to run the following command:

```
ember build --environment="production"
```

This will build the application for the production environment, and put the resulting files in the `dist` directory of your project. In order to build your project in a different location, you can specify the output path using `--output-path` flag, to specify the directory where you want to build the project.

Now the contents present in the `dist` directory can be deployed, as it is to your application server.

Ember CLI also makes it very easy to deploy your application to Heroku.

To deploy your application to Heroku, run the following command in your project's root directory:

```
heroku create <OPTIONAL_APP_NAME> --buildpack https://github.com/
tonycoco/heroku-buildpack-ember-cli.git
```

After this, you should be able to deploy your application to Herkoku using the usual `git` hooks:

```
git commit -am "Commit to deploy to heroku" --allow-empty
git push heroku master
```

To run any of the commands, you will need a Heroku account and its toolbelt set up on your machine.

Migrating existing Ember applications to Ember CLI

In order to migrate an existing Ember.js application to an Ember CLI-compatible application, the first thing you need to do is to install Ember CLI in the project's root folder using the following command:

```
npm install –save-dev ember-cli
```

This should add a `package.json` file in your project's root, with Ember CLI as its dependency.

Now you should be able to run the `ember` command from the project's root directory.

The next step is to initialize an empty Ember CLI application using the `ember init` command.

Running the `ember init` command will initialize an empty Ember CLI, the same structure we discussed in the section, *Creating a new application*. It will also install the bower and node dependencies automatically, like the `ember new` command.

When `ember init` finishes, you should run the `ember server` to start the development server, if you see the appropriate **Welcome to Ember.js** screen. This means that the project has been initialized properly.

The main task left now is to make your code compatible with Ember CLI's resolver, which resolves different components based on the ES6 module. It is exported from a file whose name is based on Ember.js conventions.

Without Ember CLI	With Ember CLI
```App.IndexRoute =Ember.Route.extend({ model: function() { return ['something','else']; }});```	```// app/routes/index.jsimport Ember from 'ember'export default Ember.Route.extend({ model: function(){ return ["something","else"]; }});```

Here are some of the things that should be paid some attention while converting your exiting application to Ember CLI:

- Ember CLI uses a custom resolver, which uses different conventions to resolve Ember.js components. Earlier a resolver was used to resolve components from the global namespace, like `App`. Ember CLI uses a resolver that resolves components from the ES6 compatible modules that are exported from the different files present in their designated folder. For example, post controller will be resolved from the module that is exported from the `post.js` file, present inside `<your-application>/app/controllers/post.js`, instead of `App.PostController`.

- The script tag no longer surrounds the `.hbs` or `handlebars.js` templates. The templates are automatically compiled from the `<your-application>/app/templates/` location. Here too, the name of the template file should match with that of the route, or the template that is used elsewhere.

- Remember to always import Ember with `import Ember from "ember";`.

- Ember CLI makes it easy to import third-party libraries using bower. You will have to add the necessary import statements in `Brofile.js`, in order for these libraries to be made available to the application, via the broccoli asset pipeline.

- To include the libraries that can't be installed via bower, you can put them in a `vendor` directory, and import them to broccoli.

Code samples used in this book

Now that we have got a good introduction to Ember.js with Ember CLI, let's see how can you access and run the code samples used in this book. You can find all the code samples of this book on GitHub at https://github.com/suchitpuri/emberjs-essentials.

> Previous knowledge of using the Git distributed version control system is required to clone and fork the repository. To learn more about Git, please refer to http://git-scm.com/book/en/v2/Getting-Started-Git-Basics or https://try.github.io/levels/1/challenges/1.

There is a separate folder for every chapter inside the emberjs-essentials repository. Inside every chapter, you will find examples for that chapter. Each example is a separate Ember CLI project.

In order to clone and run an example from the GitHub repository, please run the following command at the location where you want to check out the emberjs-essentials repository:

```
git clone git@github.com:suchitpuri/emberjs-essentials.git
```

After this, you will find the code for the book being checked out inside the emberjs-essentials directory.

You will need to install Ember CLI on your machine to run the code examples of this book. To install and understand Ember CLI, please refer to the *Prerequisites* section, inside *Setting up your first Ember.js application using Ember CLI*.

Once Ember CLI and its dependencies are installed, navigate to the example you want to run, and run the ember install command:

```
cd emberjs-essentials/chapter-2/example1/
```

```
ember install
```

ember install will install the dependencies of the project by running bower install and npm install.

To start the development server here, run the following command:

```
ember server
```

This should start the development server at `http://localhost:4200/`.

Now you can open the above location in the browser of your choice and see your example.

Summary

In this chapter, we learnt about the evolution of web applications. We saw how well designed the Ember.js framework is. It tries to bring proven design principles and patterns into the realm of single page web applications. The framework lets you focus on building the core business logic of your application, as it takes care of everything else behind the scenes.

We learned about Ember CLI, and how it brings in a lot of tools and builds processes to solve most of the problems faced while developing and deploying an Ember.js application. We also learned how we can migrate an existing Ember.js application to Ember CLI, followed by how to access and run the code samples used in this book.

This chapter also gives a short description of the different layers of the Ember.js framework, and as we proceed through the chapters, we will get into the details of these components. We will see how effective and elegant Ember.js is in solving some of the most common and unique problems of single page web applications.

2
Understanding Ember.js Object-oriented Patterns

JavaScript is a multi paradigm dynamic language that supports all of the object-oriented, procedural, and functional styles of writing code. This makes it one of the most powerful, as well as the most misunderstood language of all times.

Often one aims to write code that is modular, extensible, and testable. But not everyone is able to write good quality code because it requires deep understanding of the language, design principles, as well as discipline to write code that consistently follows a particular school of thought.

Ember.js framework helps in creating applications which are highly modular, extensible, and can be tested easily, and the Ember object model lies in the heart this framework.

In this chapter, we shall cover the following topics:

- Ember.js object model
- Reuse functions via mixins
- Bindings
- Computed properties
- Observers
- Prototype add on helpers

Ember.js object model

Almost all of the objects in Ember are derived from `Ember.Object`. This serves as the base object of models, views, controllers, and even the application. Hence, it is also responsible for consistency across the application, adding in similar capabilities to all the objects.

Most of the popular object-oriented languages such as Ruby, Java, C#, and Python follow classical inheritance patterns. These languages have a concept of classes and objects. Classes define the properties and behavior. Objects are instances of these classes. For inheritance to work, classes inherit properties and behavior from other classes.

JavaScript, on the other hand follows a prototypal inheritance pattern instead of the classical inheritance pattern. JavaScript has no concept of classes. It has objects, and objects inherit properties and behavior from other objects. Going forward, this might change with the release of ECMAScript 6 JavaScript standard (http://wiki.ecmascript.org/doku.php?id=harmony:specification_drafts). We might see "class" and classical inheritance features built in the language itself.

Ember.js tries to bridge this gap in JavaScript prototypal inheritance, and the classical inheritance by providing a library that emulates classical inheritance. This makes it easy for developers working in languages supporting classical inheritance to pick up Ember.js patterns really quickly and easily.

For example, in JavaScript if you had to implement a simple form of inheritance, you could do the following:

```
var base = { baseProperty: true }
var derived = Object.create(base)
console.log(derived.baseProperty) // true
```

In Ember.js, if you had to do the same, that is implement a simple form of inheritance, you would do the following:

```
var base = Ember.Object.extend({
  baseProperty: true
});

var derived = base.extend({
  derivedProperty:false
});

var derivedObject = derived.create();

console.log(derivedObject.get('baseProperty'));
console.log(derivedObject.get('derivedProperty'));
```

To run the above example using Ember CLI, let's create a new file `inheritance.js` inside the project's `app` directory. In our case, that would be `chapter-2/example1/app/inheritance.js`.

Now, since the general convention used in Ember CLI is to export your ECMAScript 6 module, and then import the same wherever you want to use it by using the `import` keyword. Lets first create and export our module, which will contain the preceding JavaScript and Ember.js inheritance code.

```
import Ember from 'ember';
export default function(){
  // Using Plain JavaScript
  console.log("using plain JavaScript");
  var base = {
    baseProperty: true
  };
  var derived = Object.create(base);
  console.log(derived.baseProperty);

  // Using Ember.js
  console.log("using Ember.js");
  var base = Ember.Object.extend({
    baseProperty: true
  });

  var derived = base.extend({
    derivedProperty:false
  });

  var derivedObject = derived.create();

  console.log(derivedObject.get('baseProperty'));
  console.log(derivedObject.get('derivedProperty'));
}
```

The contents of inheritance.js are present in chapter-2/example1/app/inheritance.js

You can see that we have wrapped our code inside a JavaScript function that is exported from the file. Since we would want to use the `Ember.Object.extend`, we import the `Ember` module using:

```
import Ember from 'ember'
```

Now the only part remaining is to include our inheritance module, inside `app.js` present inside the project's `app` directory, for the example that would be `chapter-2/example1/app/app.js`. So let's add the following line inside the `app.js` file:

```
import inheritance from './inheritance';
```

Doing this will import the exported module from `app/inheritance.js`, and assign the module to the local variable named `inheritance`.

Now we can just call our exported function using `inheritance()`, inside `app/app.js`.

To run the example, navigate to the `chapter-2/example1` folder and run the following commands in the same order:

npm install

bower install

ember serve

This should start the development server at `http://localhost:4200/`. Open the `http://localhost:4200/` location in your browser, and you should see **Welcome to Ember.js** on your screen.

 Once all the dependencies are installed, you can run your development server with only `ember serve` command. This should work fine unless you change any of your project dependencies.

In order to see the console log, open the development tools of your browsers and open the console to see the logs.

 Please note that we will be using the same pattern described above to create and run the rest of the example in this chapter.

Coming back to the code, let's see what is happening here:

```
var base = Ember.Object.extend({
  baseProperty: true
});
```

Here, we defined a variable `base` that inherits the properties and behavior of `Ember.Object`, using the `extend` method present in the `Ember.Object` class.

The `extend` method is a way to implement classical inheritance in Ember.js framework. `extend` behaves like a classical inheritance static method, and exists in the `Ember.Object` class. This method takes in variable arguments, starting with zero or more mixins, followed by an object containing new properties that we want to define on the object. In the above example, we did not provide any mixins and only provided the new properties we want on the class. We will be discussing more about mixins later, in the *Reuse via mixins* section of this chapter.

The `base` object extends the `Ember.Object` class. Doing this makes `base` inherit the properties and behavior from `Ember.Object`. `Ember.Object` adds in additional capabilities, such as emulating classical inheritance by using the `extend` method, bindings, observer, computed properties, and much more to the `base` object.

In a similar fashion, the `derived` object inherits its properties from the `base` object. As you can see, we have not defined any method on the `base` object and still we are able to use `base.extend({})`. This is because when a method is called on an object, the object looks for its definition in its defining class. If the definition is not found in the class, the object will look for the definition in the superclass, this process continues till a matching definition is found.

In the next step, we create an instance of the `derived` class using the `derived.create()` method. The `create` method is inherited from the `Ember.Object` class, and it returns a new instance of the class, which is `derived` in our case.

The `create` method also takes in an optional argument object containing the properties we want to initialize on the object. It is important to understand the difference between `create` and `extend`. The `extend` method is used to extend the behavior and properties of an existing class to define a new one, it does not create any instances of the definition. The `create` method, on the other hand, is used to create an instance of a defined class.

Let's see another, a bit more complex example of the above inheritance code. The following example can be found in `chapter-2/example2/` directory:

```
import Ember from 'ember';
export default function(){

  var base = Ember.Object.extend({
    baseProperty: true
  });

  var derived = base.extend({});

  var derviedObject = derived.create({
    derivedProperty: true
```

```
  });

  console.log(derviedObject.get('baseProperty'));//true
  console.log(derviedObject.get('derivedProperty'));//true

  var anotherDerivedObject = derived.create();
  console.log(anotherDerivedObject.get('derivedProperty'));
  //undefined
}
```

The contents of inheritance2.js are present in chapter-2/example2/app/inheritance2.js

As you can see that when we pass in the argument object to the `create` method, it adds those properties only to the newly instantiated object and not to the class definition:

```
var derviedObject = derived.create({
  derivedProperty: true
});
```

The `derivedProperty`, which we will add on the `derivedObject`, will be accessible on to only this object and hence, any other instances of type `derived` will not be able to access the `derivedPoperty` property, and will return `undefined` for the same.

In order to add a property that is accessible to all the instances of the class, we need to either define the property, when we define the class, as shown:

```
var derived = base.extend({
  derivedProperty: true
});
```

Or you can also use the `reopen` method, once you have defined the class using the `extend` method:

```
import Ember from 'ember';

export default function(){

  var base = Ember.Object.extend({
    baseProperty: true
  });

  var derived = base.extend({
  });

  derived.reopen({
    derivedProperty: true
```

```
    });

    var derviedObject = derived.create({
    });

    console.log(derviedObject.get('baseProperty'));//true
    console.log(derviedObject.get('derivedProperty'));//true

    var anotherDerivedObject = derived.create();
    console.log(anotherDerivedObject.get('derivedProperty'));//true
}
```

The contents of inheritance3.js are present in chapter-2/example3/app/inheritance3.js

The `reopen` method is particularly useful when you want to modify the class definition after it has been defined. Once the `reopen` method is called, all new instances of the class will have the additional properties.

Reuse via mixins

As we saw in the above examples, JavaScript objects can inherit properties from other objects. The inherited object can also inherit properties and behavior from other objects, thus forming an inheritance chain. While sometimes it makes sense to represent the object hierarchy in terms of their natural order, but a lot of other times it also becomes messy and unmanageable to handle long inheritance chains. Thankfully, when it comes to alternatives for function reuse, JavaScript makes it possible to implement the mixin reuse design pattern.

In computer science, a **mixin** is a class, which contains the behavior for a particular type (shape, color, person). Mixins are supposed to contain the behavior, or verbs, rather than the properties, or nouns. They are considered to be abstract, which means that they are not intended to be instantiated on their own, but they are supposed to lend or copy their methods or behavior to the borrowing class. Using mixins can be thought of as using composition, rather than inheritance.

Ember.js makes it really easy to implement and use this design pattern. Ember CLI follows the convention of putting the mixins in the `app/mixins/` directory of your project.

Let's create two mixins, a focusable mixin and a number validator mixin present in the `app/mixins/` directory. The code for this example can be found inside `chapter-2/example4/` directory:

```
import Ember from 'ember';

export default Ember.Mixin.create({
```

```
    valid: function(number){
      if(isNaN(number)){
        return false;
      }else{
        return true;
      }
    }
});
```

The contents of valid_number.js are present in chapter-2/example4/app/mixins/valid_number.js

```
import Ember from 'ember';

export default Ember.Mixin.create({
  onFocus: function(){
    console.log("do something creative on focus");
  }
});
```

The contents of focusable.js are present in chapter-2/example4/app/mixins/focusable.js

```
App.NumericTextBox =
  Ember.Object.extend(App.ValidNumberMixin,App.FocusableMixin,{
    text:""
});
var textbox = App.NumericTextBox.create();
console.log(textbox.valid("12")); //true
textbox.onFocus(); //do something creative on focus
```

As you can see that we define a new mixin in Ember.js using the `Ember.Mixin.create` statement, `Ember.Mixin` class serves as a base for all the mixins you would be creating in your Ember.js application. Since `Ember.Mixin` class cannot extend other mixins, there is no `extend` method on the `Ember.Mixin` class. There is only a `create` method that is used to instantiate the `Ember.Mixin` class with the supplied behavior.

After we have defined two mixin instances, `validNumberMixin` and `focusableMixin`, each having their own functionality; lets create the `numerictBox` object that includes the above two mixins.

```
import Ember from 'ember';
import validNumberMixin from './mixins/valid_number';
import focusableMixin from './mixins/focusable';

export default Ember.Object.extend(validNumberMixin,focusableMixin,{
  text:""
});
```

The contents of numeric_box.js are present in chapter-2/app/numeric_box.js

Here, you can see that we have exported an object that extends from `Ember.Object` in our file. Since the mixins are not available by default to our module, we will have to import them explicitly using the `import` keyword.

As we discussed earlier, the `extend` method present in `Ember.Object` also takes in optional arguments of `Ember.Mixin` type. By including these mixins, we are copying the behavior present in the mixins to our `validNumberMixin` definition. Thus, calling `valid` and `onFocus` on the instance of `numericBox`, should work as expected.

Let's now call the `numericBox` from `app/app.js`, in order for our code to run when the application initializes:

```
import numbeicBox from './numeric_box';

var textbox = numbeicBox.create();
console.log(textbox.valid("12"));//true
textbox.onFocus();// do something creative on focus"
```

Mixins provide a very interesting alternative to simplifying your JavaScript inheritance chain. This pattern makes it easy when you want to inherit properties from more than once source, thus simplifying your code bases while keeping functionality in independent testable units.

Computed properties

Objects in JavaScript are a combination of data (or properties), and behavior (or methods). It can also be thought as a key value store, wherein keys are the names of the properties and values containing the data or methods. You can access plain JavaScript properties by using either the dot notation or the bracket notation as follows:

```
var obj = { firstName: "suchit", lastName:"puri"};
console.log(obj.firstName); //Dot Notation
console.log(obj['lastName']); //Bracket Notation
```

Getter and setter methods

In order to provide features like property bindings, computed properties, auto updating templates, and a lot more, Ember.js framework uses `get` and `set` methods, instead of accessing the properties directly, as shown above. These methods, apart from returning and setting the properties on the object, also register property changes in the object, and will trigger any listeners that are observing this property:

```
var emberObject = Ember.Object.create({
    firstName:"suchit",
```

```
    lastName: "puri"
});
console.log(emberObject.get('firstName')); //suchit
emberObject.set('firstName',"something");
console.log(emberObject.get('firstName')); //something
```

The `set` method also lets you chain your setters. You could do something like the following:

```
emberObject.set('firstName',"something").set('lastName',
    "anything").get("firstName");
```

Such chaining of method calls can be really handy in `seeding/changing` data, while writing the test cases for `Ember.Object` instances.

Sometimes, instead of just using plain properties, you might want to transform or aggregate the data present in them. Computed properties in Ember.js let you use your functions as properties, so that you can add the logic to transform the data present in other properties. You can use `get` method to get the computed property, like any other property. Let's take a look at the following example:

```
import Ember from 'ember';

export default Ember.Object.extend({
    firstName: "",
    lastName: "",
    fullName: function(){
        return this.get('firstName') + " " + this.get('lastName');
    }.property('firstName','lastName')
});
```

The contents of user.js are present in chapter-2/example5/app/user.js

Getting the user properties from `app.js` present in `chapter-2/example5/app/app.js` as follows:

```
import user from './user';

myUser = user.create({
    firstName: "suchit",
    lastName: "puri"
});
console.log(myUser.get('fullName')); //suchit puri
```

Here, as you can see, we have defined a `user` class. In this definition, we have defined a method `fullName` that returns the combination of your first name and last name. The only distinguishing factor about the `fullName` method is that we have explicitly made this function to act as a property, by appending the property at the end.

The `property` method makes a normal function act like an Ember.js object property. The arguments of the `property` method make the function dependent on other properties, which means that if any of the properties present in the arguments of the `property` method changes, the function recomputes its value.

Let's see that in the following example:

```
import Ember from 'ember';

export default Ember.Object.extend({
  firstName: "",
  lastName: "",
  fullName: function(){
    return this.get('firstName') + " " + this.get('lastName');
  }.property('firstName','lastName')
});
```

The contents of user.js are present in chapter-2/example5/app/user.js

Getting/setting the `user` properties from `app.js` is present in `chapter-2/example5/app/app.js`, as follows:

```
import user from './user';

myUser = user.create({
  firstName: "suchit",
  lastName: "puri"
});

console.log(myUser.get('fullName')); //suchit puri
myUser.set("firstName","Tony");
myUser.set("lastName","Stark");
console.log(myUser.get('fullName'));//Tony Stark
```

If, after fetching in the full name, we decide to change the first name and last name of our `user` object, we can do this by using the set function on our object. The next time we go to fetch the `fullName`, we will get the updated `fullName` of the user.

One important thing to note is that all the computed properties are cached by default, which means that once you request the computed property, the framework will compute it and cache it for you. The framework will only call the function again if any of the properties it is dependent on changes.

Let's take a look at the following example:

```
import Ember from 'ember';

export default Ember.Object.extend({
  firstName: "",
  lastName: "",
  fullName: function(){
    console.log("fullName computed property called");
    return this.get('firstName') + " " + this.get('lastName');
  }.property('firstName','lastName')
});
```

The contents of user.js are present in chapter-2/example6/app/user.js

```
import user from './user';

var myUser = user.create({
  firstName: "suchit",
  lastName: "puri"
});

console.log(myUser.get('fullName'));
myUser.set("firstName","Tony");
myUser.set("lastName","Stark");
console.log(myUser.get('fullName'));
console.log(myUser.get('fullName'));

//Output

//"fullName computed property called"
//"suchit puri"
//"fullName computed property called"
//"Tony Stark"
//"Tony Stark"
```

The contents of app.js are present in chapter-2/example6/app/app.js

Let us have a look at the example:

1. Here, we are first calling the `fullName` computed property on the `user` object, whose first name is `suchit` and last name is `puri`. Doing this, the function `fullName` is executed, which can be verified by seeing the console log statement `"fullName computed property called"`. The full name of the user is printed as expected.

2. Now let's change the `firstName` and `lastName` attributes of the user by using `user.set`, and get the new `fullName` of the user. Again, we can verify the console log statement getting printed, followed by the correct full name. Here, we see that since the first name and last name of the user were changed, the cache for the computed property was invalidated. When we called the full name computed property on the user object, the function was called again, and returned the correct full name of the user.

3. Let us now call the `fullName` computed property again, without changing the `firstName` and `lastName` of the user. You can see in the output that the console log statement never gets printed. Since none of the dependent properties of `fullName` will change the framework, we will use the cached value of the computed property.

The key thing to understand here is that you need to include all the dependent properties correctly, while creating your computed property. Failing to do so will mean that the computed property will not return the correct results and will be using stale cached values.

Let's see that by an example, the `chapter-2/example7/`:

```
import Ember from 'ember';

export default Ember.Object.extend({
  firstName: "",
  lastName: "",
  fullName: function(){
    console.log("fullName computed property called");
    return this.get('firstName') + " " + this.get('lastName');
  }.property('lastName')
});
```

The contents of user.js are present in chapter-2/example7/app/user.js

```
import user from './user';

var myUser = user.create({
  firstName: "suchit",
  lastName: "puri"
```

```
});

console.log(myUser.get('fullName'));
myUser.set("firstName","Tony");
console.log(myUser.get('fullName'));

//output
//"fullName computed property called"
//"suchit puri"
//"suchit puri"
```

The contents of app.js are present in chapter-2/example7/app/app.js

Here, we have removed the `firstName` dependency from our computed property `fullName`. Now `fullName` depends only on the `lastName`. Doing this, the cache of computed property would only get invalidated, if the last name changes.

Let us get the `fullName` of the user. We can see in the output that it returns the correct result. It calls in the function `fullName`, which returns the correct full name of the user. Now, if we update the `firstName` of the user, and call the `fullName` computed property on the user, it will still return the earlier cached value `suchit puri`, since none of the dependent property of the computed property has changed. You can see that such small things can result in unexpected behavior in your application. So, as a rule of thumb, include all the properties a computed property uses as dependent properties.

Observers in Ember.js

Observers in Ember.js are methods that observe one or more object properties and are called when these properties change.

At first, they may seem similar to computed properties, but in reality they are completely different from them. One very big difference being that computed properties are functions which behave like normal properties that can be accessed via, `get` and `set` methods, and can be used in templates like any other property.

Observers on other hand are like listeners in JavaScript. They observe properties, and get called when these properties changes. They cannot be accessed like properties neither can they be used in templates. Let us see an example of observer `chapter-2/example8`:

```
import Ember from 'ember';

export default Ember.Object.extend({
  time:00,
```

```
  timeChanged: function(){
    //Do something when time changes
    console.log('time changed');
  }.observes('time')
});
```

The contents of time_manager.js are present in chapter-2/example8/app/time_manager.js

```
import timeManager from './time_manager';

var myTimeManager = timeManager.create({
  time: 12
});

myTimeManager.set("time",22);

//Output
//time changed
```

Time manager being used in app.js is present in chapter2/example8/app/app.js

Here, we have created a time manager, which has a property called as `time`. We have created an observer, `timeChanged`, which monitors the `time` property. Whenever the `time` property changes, the observer is fired. `myTimeManager` is an instance of `timeManager`. Let's change the time of `myTimeManager` and see if the observer is fired or not. If you run the above code, you will see that `time changed` is printed on the console.

As `timeChanged` is an observer and not a property, if you try and get the property `timeChanged` on the object, you will get the function instead of the property. You can also manually invoke the observer by using `myTimeManager.timeChanged()`, just like any other method.

 One important thing to note here is that observers are fired only after the object is fully initialized. If we want an observer to fire during the object initialization, we can instruct the framework to do that too.

In the above code, the observer is fired only after you change the `time` property, using the `set` method. If we want the observer to be called even when the object was initializing, we can do that by using `observes('time').on('init')`. Doing this will trigger the observer twice; once during the object creation and initialization, and second time when we change the value of `time` property by using `set`.

Bindings across objects

Till now, we have seen bindings and dependencies between the properties of one object. Ember.js provides you with the ability to take those dependencies across objects. There could be cases wherein the properties of one object depend on the properties of another object. In such a case, Ember.js bindings come really handy.

Let us see that in the following example, `chapter-2/example9/`:

```
import Ember from 'ember';

export default Ember.Object.extend({
  name: "",
  age:18,
  address:"",
});
```

The contents of father.js are present in chapter-2/example9/app/father.js

```
import Ember from 'ember';

export default Ember.Object.extend({
  school:'',
  father:null,
  address: Ember.computed.alias('father.address')
});
```

The contents of child.js are present in chapter-2/example9/app/father.js

```
import father from './father';
import child from './child';

var darren = father.create({
  name:'Darren',
  age:40,
  address:'Brisbane'
});

var dan = child.create({
  school:'Brisbane State High School',
```

```
      father: darren
});

console.log(dan.get('address'));

darren.set('address','Sydney')

console.log(dan.get('address'));

//Output
//Brisbane
//Sydney
```

The father and child classes being used in app.js are present in chapter-2/example9/app/app.js

Here we have created two object types, a `father` and a `child` type. You can see in the `child` definition that the address of a child is same as its father's. Ember.js helps you to create bindings like this, which are between objects. Now, since the address of the child depends on the address of the father, when we update the address of the father, the changes reflect automatically in the child object as well. As a result, when use `dan.get(address)`, it returns the correct address, which is `sydney`.

Prototype extensions

To make your life simpler, Ember.js framework extends the prototypes of `Array`, `String`, `Function` are native JavaScript objects. These extensions provide you with simpler ways of accessing and manipulating these native objects.

As for arrays, you could do the following:

```
export default function(){
  console.log([1,2,3].get('lastObject')); //4

  var arr = [1,2,3,4,5,6,7].filter(function(item){
    if(item < 5){
      return true;
    }
  });
  console.log(arr);//[1,2,3,4]
}
```

The contents of prototype.js are present in chapter-2/example10/app/prototype.js

For strings, you could do the following:

```
console.log("ember.js".capitalize()); //Ember.js
console.log("my var".camelize());//myVar
console.log("my var".classify());//MyVar
```

> For a complete list of `Array` helper methods, please refer to the API documentation, found at `http://emberjs.com/api/classes/Ember.Array.html`.
>
> Similarly, for `String` helper please see the API documentation, found at `http://emberjs.com/api/classes/Ember.String.html`.

These function prototype extensions will help you to use getters, setters, computed properties, observers, and much more. Examples of computed properties, bindings, and observers fit well here.

Summary

In this chapter, we learned about the Ember.js object model. This philosophy and style of writing code is core to building good Ember.js single page web applications. To understand the framework properly, it is very important to get hold of these concepts. We also looked at the computed properties and observers used in Ember. js. We also covered about the various helper methods that Ember.js adds to strings, arrays, and functions to make our life simpler. Then, we looked at bindings in Ember.js, and how they help us maintain sync between different properties and objects. In the end, we learned briefly about the prototypal extensions Ember.js provides, and how they let you easily solve some common tasks.

In the next chapter, we will learn about handlebars, templates, syntax, and nuances. We will see how Ember.js uses these concepts to create beautiful auto-updating view templates.

3
Rendering Using Templates

In the last chapter, you learned about Ember.js object-oriented design choices. In this chapter, you will learn about the Ember.js presentation layer. You will see how to use Handlebars.js, the default template processor in Ember.js.

In this chapter, we shall cover the following areas:

- An introduction to JavaScript templates using Handlebars.js
- HTMLBars and Handlebars
- Defining a Handlebars.js template
- Handlebars.js expressions
- Handlebars.js conditionals
- Displaying a list of items using Handlebars.js
- Binding HTML tag attributes
- Action event bubbling
- Handlebars.js input helpers
- Building custom Handlebars.js helpers
- Using the concise Emblem.js templating language

An introduction to JavaScript templates using Handlebars.js

Traditionally, presentation template systems have been used mostly on the server side. Be it Jade, StringTemplate or any other template engine, they have helped us separate the business logic from the presentation logic. They have made our code more reusable, and easy to understand and test.

With a gradual shift in today's web application, more and more logic is now shifting from server side to client side. Single-page web applications are a perfect example of that. To give users a perfect immersive experience, single-page web applications handle most of the logic related to the user's interaction at client side.

One of the most common challenges faced in giving that immersive experience is how to gracefully update the UI of the application whenever the user interacts with it.

There are a quite a few ways of doing that. Let's see some of them:

- Let the server send the complete HTML partial as a response to a request. This means that whenever a single-page web application requests a resource from the server, the server sends in the data wrapped in HTML to the client. I am sure you can figure out a lot of issues with this approach. Let me highlight the main ones as follows:
  - Doing this will result in a code that is tightly coupled with the way it is presented to an end user. Such a code is very brittle and is not open to changes.
  - Since the code is tightly coupled with the presentation layer, code reusability is reduced.

- The other possibility would be to send the data in either JSON or any other non-verbose format. Then, use JavaScript to mix the received data with HTML and update the **Document Object Model (DOM)** with the latest data. We now have better decoupling between the data and presentation logic, the server now talks in raw JSON data, and the client decorates it with HTML and presents it to the end user. Though we have increased the decoupling between the data and presentation logic, it is still not ideal because now JavaScript functions are burdened with the responsibility of mixing the DOM with the data returned from the server. Consider the following method, which is called as a success callback of an AJAX call:

```
functionupdateDom(data) {
  varlist = $("ul");
  var comment = "<li><span>" + data.name + "</span>" +
    "<div>" + data.comment "</div></li>";
  list.append(newComment);
}
```

For small applications that have fewer presentation changes, this should be fine. But as the application grows, this makes the JavaScript code more and more complex and difficult to maintain.

- Let's look at the third, and even better, way of updating the UI templates with the latest data from the server. The only problem we noticed in the last approach was that we had to manually write in JavaScript functions to mix the HTML with the data returned from the server, which we figured out is not scalable, as the functions to update the UI will get more and more complex as the UI evolves. Wouldn't it be much better if we could write reusable UI templates separately and just add placeholders for the data that has to be displayed in it? Something like the following:

```
<li>
  <p class="name">Hello This is {{ data.name }}</p>
  <p>I live at {{ data.address }}</p>
</li>
```

  The biggest advantage we got out of this approach is that we have now decoupled the data and the UI, to a large extent. The frontend developer can now work on the UI parallel, using plain HTML. They just need to add placeholders for the data to be displayed. The server responds in JSON and is agnostic to the UI that is consuming the data. The same response could be used by a mobile application to build its UI. Now, the only thing that we're left with is to implement the JavaScript, which replaces or binds the placeholders present in the templates with actual data.

Handlebars.js does what has just been mentioned in the third point and much more. Since today's ambitious web applications have much more complex UI and workflows, you would need a template engine that takes care of segregating the UI logic from the business logic of your application.

Harndlerbars.js is a semantic web template system, which was started in 2010 by Yahuda Katz. Handlebars.js is essentially a compiler that takes in the HTML with placeholders in it and outputs a JavaScript method. This compiled JavaScript method takes in argument for the data and returns the string containing your HTML with actual data. But all this is hidden from an end user and is taken care by the Ember. js framework in the backend. You just need to define the template with the correct convention and things should work fine.

HTMLBars and Handlebars

When Ember.js framework was being built, the team did not just pick up **mustache** templates (found at `http://mustache.github.io/`) and integrate with Ember.js. Mustache is logic-less templating library whose implementation is available in over 37 different languages, including JavaScript. Handlebars.js was built from scratch to support data binding and other Ember.js features. Handlebars.js has been improving since then and has been quite stable over the years. But recently in 2014, Yahuda Katz and the team wanted to improve Handlebars.js even further. These improvements changed the way Handlebars.js was being used inside Ember.js. So, instead of releasing the next version of Handlebars.js, the team decided to release a completely new project called as HTMLBars.

HTMLBars is the new templating library and will be enabled by default starting Ember.js 1.10 and Ember.js 1.11 beta. It is built on top of Handlebars.js and is backward compatible with its syntax. HTMLBars' biggest difference with Handlebars.js is that it builds DOM elements instead of string and hence it is said to be at least 30% faster than Handlebars.js.

The following image explains how does the Handlebars.js template system works:

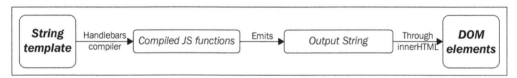

The Handlebars.js working flow

The following image explains how HTMLBars simplifies things by directly emitting DOM elements instead strings:

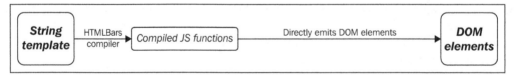

The HTMLBars working flow

To easily upgrade to Ember.js 1.10 and HTMLBars, the Ember CLI users should update the Ember CLI to version 0.1.12 or later.

It is very important to note here that whatever syntax we will discuss in this chapter will be applicable to both Handlebars.js as well as HTMLBars.js and should work in both the cases.

Defining templates

Let's see how templates fit in to our Ember.js application. When you create a new application using Ember CLI, you will find the `app/templates` folder inside your application. This is where the Ember.js resolver looks for template files for your project.

Let's look at the default `application.hbs` template present at `app/templates/`:

```
<h2 id="title">Welcome to Ember.js</h2>
{{outlet}}
```

The default application template is present at chapter-3/example1/app/templates/application.hbs

The application template is the main template that is rendered when the application starts. The most common use case for application templates is to put in the header and footer of the application here. This is the entry point for the application and it makes sense to put in sections of the application that will remain visible throughout the application here. All the routes that are rendered will be nested under the application route. We will talk more about the routes and naming conventions used to associate templates with model, views, and controllers in *Chapter 4, Managing Application State Using Ember.js Routes*.

The application template should also contain at least one `{{outlet}}` helper. The outlet helper tells the router to render the next appropriate template in place of the `{{outlet}}` helper. The next template is usually resolved from the routes and URL convention. We will be discussing more about the convention router in *Chapter 4, Managing Application State Using Ember.js Routes*.

Let's change the application template to include our headers and footer notes. Let's also render the following templates between header and footer by placing the `{{outlet}}` helper in between the header and footer tags:

```
<header>
  <h2>Welcome to Ember.js</h2>
</header>
<div>
  {{outlet}}
</div>
```

```
<footer>
  &copy;2014 Ember.js Essentials
</footer>
```

The modified application.hbs that now includes header and footer information is present
at chapter-3/example1/app/templates/application.hbs

As you can see, here we have moved the outlet tag between the header and footer. Let's create a new index template that now renders between the header and footer when we access the `http://localhost:4200/` URL. We will be discussing more about how the routes match and resolve the template names in *Chapter 4, Managing Application State Using Ember.js Routes*. Till then, it is safe to assume that when you open the application index \ URL in the browser, the application template is rendered, which, in turn, renders the index template in place of the `{{outlet}}` helper.

To create the index template, let's create a new file `index.hbs` inside the `app/templates/` directory with the following content:

```
<ul>
  {{#each item in model}}
    <li>{{item}}</li>
  {{/each}}
</ul>
```

The contents of index template are present in chapter-3/example1/app/templates/index.hbs

Now, if you run `chapter-3/example1` by running the `ember serve` command in the terminal and open the `http://localhost:4200/` URL in your browser, you will see the following output:

Adding a header and footer in the application template

Here, we have used a simple header and footer, but you could potentially use a more complex and better UI for your application.

Your template can also have more than one outlet. In such cases, outlets are usually named so that you can tell the router which outlet to render your template, as follows:

```
{{ outlet "sidebar"}}
```

We will be discussing more about named outlets when we discuss routes in *Chapter 4*, *Managing Application State Using Ember.js Routes*.

Handlebars.js expressions

By this time, you would have figured out that Handlebars.js expressions are wrapped in {{}}. The Ember.js framework provides us with two initial routes: the application route and index route. The application route renders the application template present at `app/templates/application.hbs` when the application initializes. The index route is activated when the users visits the / or the index of the application. It renders the index template from `app/templates/index.hbs`. If you need any custom behavior other than what's already there, you will have to provide your implementation of the routes. Template will look for data from its associated controller. "Convention Over Configuration" governs the association between a controller and template. You don't have to manually wire up things here.

In our case, the `index` template will look for data from the index controller present and exported from `app/controllers/index.js`. But we have not defined the index controller anywhere. Whenever the Ember.js framework cannot find the required component, it will try and generate one for you. In our case, even though we have not defined the index controller, the framework will not complain and generate one for you. This generated component will have the default behavior that basically does nothing. This makes our code clean and saves us from writing components that do nothing.

Let's look at the `index` template present at `chapter-3/example1/app/templates/index.hbs`:

```
<ul>
  {{#each item in model}}
  <li>{{item}}</li>
  {{/each}}
</ul>
```

You can see here that we are iterating items present in model array. Now, as we discussed above, the template will look for controller to provide the data. Now, since the "model" attribute is not present in the default index controller implementation, it should be set externally from somewhere else.

Let's look at the index route present at `chapter-3/example1/app/routes/index.js`:

```
import Ember from 'ember';

export default Ember.Route.extend({
  model: function() {
    return ['red', 'yellow', 'blue'];
  }
});
```

You can see here that we are returning an array containing three colors, `['red', 'yellow', 'blue']`, from the `model` method. Doing this, the framework will automatically set the `model` property on the corresponding index controller to `['red', 'yellow', 'blue']`.

That's why we do the following:

```
{{#each item in model}}
<li>{{item}}</li>
{{/each}}
```

In the `index` template, the `model` property is fetched from the `index` controller that is set from the index route by the framework.

Normally, a `model` method would return the data that was fetched from the server and the properties that don't have to be persisted to the server and are part of the controller definition.

Here, if we wanted to access some properties that are part of the controller, we will be accessing them directly by their name in the template. Let's see this in an example.

Now, since we want to access custom properties from the controller, we will have to define them first, as shown in the following:

```
import Ember from 'ember';

export default Ember.Controller.extend({
  name: "Suchit Puri"
});
```

The index controller present at chapter-3/example1/app/controller/index.js

Here, we have defined a `name` property in the `index` controller of our application; let's change the template to use this property, as shown in the following:

```
Hi, this is {{name}}.
    I like the following colors.
<ul>
    {{#each item in model}}
<li>{{item}}</li>
    {{/each}}
</ul>
</script>
```

The index template of our application using properties from the controller, the index template can be found at chapter-3/example1/app/templates/index.hbs

Here, you can see that when we use {{name}} in the template, it will look for that property in the index controller, which would return the correct name. Now, the `name` property present in the `index` template is bound to the template, which means that if you change the `name` property of `index` controller, the change will automatically be reflected in the template.

Now, since the basics for Handlebars.js expressions are clear, let's jump into the detailed syntax of the Handlebars.js template and see how easy it is to create custom templates for your application.

Handlebars.js conditionals

Handlebars.js does not promote the use of complex business logic inside your templates. It makes it difficult to mix complex business logic in the templates by providing a very limited set of helper and scope methods. This makes your templates very clean and decoupled from the business logic.

Using complex business logic in your templates makes them very difficult to understand and debug. In any case, writing business logic in templates is a bad design choice and violates the **separation of concerns** (**SoC**) design principle, which states: "In computer science, separation of concerns (SoC) is a design principle for separating a computer program into distinct sections, such that each section addresses a separate concern."

Let's look at the `if`, `else`, and `unless` conditionals in Handlebars.js.

If, else, and unless

Frequently you will run into situations where in you would want to show or hide part of the template based on some condition that returns a boolean result. Handlebars.js conditionals are made exactly for the same purpose. The `if` conditional is a Handlebars.js helper method, which will execute the code block enclosing it when the condition is true, `else` will render the contents of the `else` block. Let's see this by looking at the following example:

```
{{#if edit}}
<ul>
  {{#each item in model}}
  <li>{{item}}</li>
  {{/each}}
</ul>
{{/if}}

<button {{action 'changeEdit'}}>Toggle</button>
```

The index template is present at chapter-3/example2/app/templates/index.hbs

As you can see in the preceding code, we have moved the earlier content of the index template of `example1` inside the `if` condition. We have also added a toggle button that will toggle the property of the `edit` flag when the button is clicked. We are using the `{{action}}` helper method to trigger an event on the click of the button. We will be talking more about the `{{action}}` helper later in this chapter, but till then it's safe to assume that on clicking the button will trigger an action `changeEdit` on the `index` controller.

Let's look at `index` controller next; as we discussed in the previous sections, a controller backs the respective template to supply the bound properties. So, in order to support the preceding `index` template, we will have to define the actions and properties inside the index controller that can then be used inside the template, as shown in the following:

```
import Ember from 'ember';


export default Ember.ObjectController.extend({
  edit: true,
  actions:{
    changeEdit: function(){
```

```
    this.toggleProperty('edit');
  }
 }
});
```

The index controller is present at chapter-2/example2/app/controller/index.js

As you can see, the index controller has an `edit` property set to `true`. It also has an `actions` object that contains the implementation of our custom actions. This implementation is called whenever the user uses the `{{action}}` helper in the template.

So, whenever the user clicks on the `Toggle` button, it triggers the `changeEdit` action event, and this event triggers the `changeEdit` method in the `actions` object that toggles the `edit` property of the controller. Now, since the template is bound to the `edit` property of the controller, it re-evaluates itself and show/hides the HTML present inside the `{{#if}}` `{{/if}}` block.

An `if` block can conditionally have an `{{else}}` block, which will execute the block when the `if` block evaluates to `false`, like any other if-else block:

```
{{#if edit}}
<!—do something here -->
{{else}}
<!—do something else here -->
{{/if}}
```

The Ember.js framework also gives you an easy syntax to check for a negative of a boolean value; so, for example, if you wanted to check if some boolean value is not true, then only execute a block, which you could do by using the `{{#unless}}` `{{/unless}}` block. The `unless` helper behaves exactly similar to the `{{#if}}` `{{/if}}` helper methods, the only difference being that it checks for the negation of the boolean value instead of the boolean value.

One interesting thing to note here is that `{{#if}}` and `{{#unless}}` are examples of block expressions, which means that these helper methods allow you to execute your helper method on a portion of template. Such helper methods in the Ember.js template system begin with # and require a closing expression to signify an end.

Displaying a list of items using Handlebars.js

One of the common use cases in today's modern web applications is showing a list of data in a tabular form. Handlebars.js allows you to easily do that via the `{{#each}}` helper.

By now, you might have observed that `index` template in `chapter-3/example1/ app/templates/index.hbs` is a classic example of iterating a list of elements. Let's see this again in the following:

```
<ul>
    {{#each item in model}}
<li>{{item}}</li>
    {{/each}}
</ul>
```

In the preceding example you can see that we are iterating over an array called as `model`. This model is set in index route, as shown in the following:

```
import Ember from 'ember';

export default Ember.Route.extend({
  model: function() {
    return ['red', 'yellow', 'blue'];
  }
});
```

When we say `{{#each item in model}}`, we are looping over all the elements present in the array `model`, and, in each iteration, we assign the current object to `item`. In our case, the `model` array contains just string names, but in real scenarios, the model can be much more complex and can contain complex JavaScript objects. Let's see this by an example: first, we need to change the index route to return a more complex object. So, instead of color names, let's return an array containing company information objects, as shown in the following:

```
import Ember from 'ember';

export default Ember.Route.extend({
  model: function() {
    var companies = [{
      "name" : "Google",
      "headquarters": "Mountain View, California,
        United States of America",
      "revenue":"59825000000"
    },{
      "name" : "Facebook",
```

```
      "headquarters":"Menlo Park, California,
        United States of America",
      "revenue":"7870000000"
    },{
      "name" : "twitter",
      "revenue": "664000000",
      "headquarters":"San Francisco, California,
        United States of America"
    }];
    return companies;
  }
});
```

The index route is present at chapter-3/example3/app/routes/index.js

Here we return an array of companies from our model function in index route, every company object is of the form:

```
{"name" : <<company name>>,"headquarters":<<headquarters>>,
"revenue":<<revenue>> }
```

Now let's create the `index` template to display the list of companies in a tabular form, as shown in the following:

```
<table id="t01">
  <tr>
    <th>Company Name</th>
    <th>Headquarters</th>
    <th>revenue</th>
  </tr>
  {{#each item in model}}
  <tr>
    <td>{{item.name}}</td>
    <td>{{item.headquarters}}</td>
    <td>{{item.revenue}}</td>
  </tr>
  {{/each}}
</table>
```

The index template is present at chapter-3/example3/app/templates/index.hbs

Here, we define a table in plain HTML markup language with our headings as Company Name, Headquarters, and revenue. Since each row in our table should display the respective company information, we will have to iterate our model array and for each record, we will have to create a new row in our table with three columns having respective data items.

Doing this will produce a table similar to that shown in the following image:

Company Information Brochure

Company Name	Headquarters	revenue
Google	Mountain View, California, United States of America	59825000000
Facebook	Menlo Park, California,United States of America	7870000000
twitter	San Francisco, California, United States of America	664000000

Iterating a complex model object

As you saw in the above example, it is easy to display a list of objects in a tabular form. You can see that the display logic is completely unaware of how to fetch the data. Like in our case, we have hardcoded the list of company information, but in a real scenario, you would be fetching the company list from a backend server. Doing this would only affect the implementation of index route's `model` method and everything else remains exactly the same.

The other benefit you get out of this approach is that the template is bound to the items present in the model array, which means that when you add or remove a company item from the model array, the view will render the company list accordingly.

Binding HTML tag attributes

In the last section, we saw how to bind values from the model object within an HTML tag. But sometimes, you may want to bind the attributes, instead of value, of an HTML tag. For example, you may want to bind the `class` attribute of a `<div>` tag because you want to style elements differently based on some logic that is accessible by the controller.

Let's see that by an example, `example4`. We will use the previous example `chapter-3/example3` as our base.

Assuming that we have a requirement to show the `headquarters` column text color based on some property in the controller. Handlebars.js allows you to do use the `{{bind-attr}}` helper method to solve such situation. The `{{bind-attr}}` method will bind the attribute name given next to a property, accessible by the controller or view:

```
<table id="t01">
  <tr>
    <th>Company Name</th>
```

```
    <th>Headquarters</th>
    <th>revenue</th>
  </tr>
  {{#each item in model}}
  <tr>
    <td>{{item.name}}</td>
    <td {{bind-attr class="className"}}>{{item.headquarters}}</td>
    <td>{{item.revenue}}</td>
  </tr>
  {{/each}}
</table>
<button {{action "toggleColor"}}> Change color </button>
```

The index template is present at chapter-3/example4/app/templates/index.hbs

As you can see in the preceding code, the only change from the previous example is that we have used the `{{bind-attr class="className"}}` helper to bind the class of headquarters column. The `{{bind-attr class="className"}}` helper, will look for `className` property in the controller to resolve the class name.

We have also added a new button at the bottom to trigger an action called `toggleColor` in the controller, whose responsibility will be to change the `className` property of the controller, based on some logic.

Till now, we have been using the default index controller, which is generated by the Ember.js framework in our examples. But now, as we need custom properties and action in our controller, we will have to explicitly define it:

```
import Ember from 'ember';

export default Ember.ObjectController.extend({
  className:"red",
  actions:{
    toggleColor: function(){
      if(this.get("className") == "red"){
        this.set("className","blue");
      }else{
        this.set("className","red");
      }
    }
  }
});
```

The index controller is present at chapter-3/example4/controllers/index.hbs

Here, you can see that we have defined a property called `className`, which will be bound to the class attribute of the `headquarters` column. We have also defined a new action, called `toggleColor`, which changes the `className` property from `red` to `blue` and vice versa.

The only thing left in our example is to define the two CSS classes, `red` and `blue`, which will set the color attribute to their respective colors. The CSS classes should be added to `chapter-3/example4/app/styles/app.css` file, as follows:

```css
.red {
color: red;
}
.blue {
color: blue
}
```

Now, when you run the above example, you will see that the `headquarters` column now is rendered in `red` color. If you press the change color button, you will notice that the `headquarters` color changes to blue. On subsequent presses, you will notice that the color toggles between red and blue.

The above example works because the `{{bind-attr class="className"}}` helper binds the controller property `className` with the class attribute of the `<td>` tag. So, whenever the `className` property of the controller changes, that change is automatically propagated to the class attribute of the `<td>` tag.

You might be thinking, why can't you just use `<td class={{controller. className}}>` or something similar, instead of using the `{{bind-attr}}` Handlebars.js helper method? The answer to the above question lies in the understanding how Ember.js tracks which section of the HTML page is to be updated when the corresponding bound property changes.

Like in our case, the Ember.js framework will have to keep track of which section of my HTML page needs to be updated when someone changes the `companies` array returned from `model` method present inside the index controller.

If you see the generated HTML of the company's table, you will find that apart from the regular `<table><tr><td>` tags, there are some additional attributes present in the `<td>` tags, something like the following:

```html
<td class="red" data-bindattr-258="258">Mountain View,
    California, United States of America</td>
```

These data bind attributes help the Ember.js framework to track which attributes to update when the corresponding bound properties in the controller changes.

Apart from `data-bindattr`, the Ember.js framework also inserts special `<script>` tags, like the following:

```
<script id="metamorph-0-start" type="text/x-placeholder"></script>
<script id="metamorph-0-end" type="text/x-placeholder"></script>.
To track the sections of HTML page it should update when the
corresponding properties changes. So as a result when you do
<td class={{item.name}}>
```

It leads to something like the following:

```
<td class="<script id="metamorph-0-start"
  type="text/x-placeholder"></script>Google
<script id="metamorph-0-end" type="text/x-placeholder"></script>"
```

This leads to HTML that is invalid and leads to an error in our code as the value of the class attribute is invalid. This is the reason we need to use special Handlebars.js helpers instead of just using `<td class={{item.name}} >`.

Ember.js team has also extracted the preceding functionality into a separate library that is called as Metamorph.js. It can be found on GitHub at `https://github.com/tomhuda/metamorph.js/`. This is particularly helpful for people who are writing their own frameworks and want to use Metamorph.js to know which sections of the page to change when their corresponding JavaScript properties changes.

Ember.js provides another workaround the above problem by using the `{{unbound}}` helper. We saw that the problem arises when the framework needs to bind the UI to JavaScript properties so that if the properties change the UI is updated accordingly. What the unbound helper does not bind the JavaScript properties to the UI and hence works fine even with the attributes; the only caveat there is that the properties are not bound to the UI and hence the UI is not updated even if the JavaScript property changes.

Action event bubbling

Handling user interaction is the core and the most important part of any modern web application. Showing, hiding, and deleting information, based on the user's interaction, is common to most web applications today.

We did the same thing in the `Company brochure` example, where we changed the color of the `headquarters` text, based on the click of a button. Though we have just changed the color of the text, but the possibilities are endless. You can show or hide elements at the click of the button, or change the full theme of the application by using the actions helper.

You may have noticed that the index template where we created a button Change Color triggers the toggleColor action on the controller:

```
<button {{action "toggleColor"}}> Change color </button>
```

You can see here that we use the {{action}} Handlebars.js helper method to trigger the action on the click of the button. Action helper can be used to make the HTML tags clickable.

When the user clicks on the element where the {{action}} helper has been used, the helper triggers an event to the controller, like in case of chapter-3/example4, the action triggers the toggleColor event to the index controller. The controller needs to define a method with the same name as the event in its action object:

```
import Ember from 'ember';
export default Ember.ObjectController.extend({
  className:"red",
  actions:{
    toggleColor: function(){
      if(this.get("className") == "red"){
        this.set("className","blue");
      }else{
        this.set("className","red");
      }
    }
  }
});
```

The index controller is present at chapter-3/example4/controllers/index.hbs

Here you can see that we have defined an actions object inside the index controller. The toggle method resides inside this actions object.

> One important thing to note here is that the component (controller or route) that handles the event triggered by the action helper should define the event handler function inside the actions object. The event will not be triggered if you define the method outside the action object.

Once the event is triggered from the DOM element, by default the event will go to the controller that is backing the template. If the controller does not implement the event handler method in its action object, the event will go to the route associated with the controller. If the route also does not implement the event handler method in its action object, it will go to the parent route and so on, till it reaches the application route.

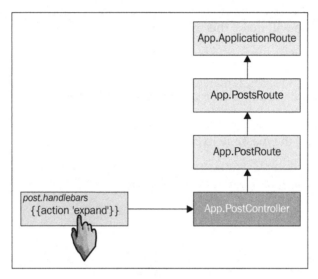

Event action bubbling

This behavior gives us the ability to handle events at different levels in our application. For example, if there are some application-wide alerts or an error message box that needs to be shown, placing the error event handler in the application route's action object will be enough to show the error message application-wide from one place.

Let us build an application-wide event handler that will show alert notifications throughout the application.

We will start with the templates first in our chapter-3/example5, starting with the application template. The example5 is an extension from example4:

```
<div {{bind-attr class="className"}}>{{message}}</div>
<h2 {{action "alert" "something went wrong form the Application
   Template"}}>Company Information Brochure</h2>
     {{outlet}}
```

The application template is present at chapter-3/example5/app/templates/application.hbs

In the following, we have added a new <div> element to house the alert:

```
<div {{bind-attr class="className"}}>{{message}}</div>
```

Here, we are using {{bind-attr}} helper to bind the class name of the div tag. The contents of the div tag will be provided by the {{message}} property from the application controller. By default, the div will be hidden, and when there is some action triggered, we will make this div visible.

Take the following line:

```
<h2 {{action "alert" "something went wrong form the Application
    Template"}}>Company Information Brochure</h2>
```

We are using the action helper to trigger an action alert on the click of the <h2> tag. We are also passing the message to be shown as an argument to the alert method.

Let's look at the application controller; the controller needs to provide the data needed by the preceding application template:

```
import Ember from 'ember';
export default Ember.ObjectController.extend({
className:"hide",
message: ""
});
```

The application controller is present at chapter-3/example5/app/controllers/application.js

Since the application template uses the className and message properties in the template, we need to serve them from the controller. So, we have set the className property to hide—this CSS class will hide the alert div. This is done so that initially nothing is visible to the user. The message property is set to an empty string, as initially there will not be any messages to show in the alert div.

Now, since we have used the {{action}} helper to trigger the alert event, we need to define an event handler for the same in either application controller or application route. As we can see that the application controller does not define any actions object, the event is bubbled up to the application route:

```
import Ember from 'ember';

export default Ember.Route.extend({
  actions:{
    alert: function(message){
      varapplicationController =
        this.controllerFor("application");
      applicationController.set("className","alert");
      applicationController.set("message",message);
```

```
Ember.run.later(function(){
  applicationController.set("className","hide");
},2000);
    }
  }
});
```

The application route is present at chapter-3/example5/app/routes/application.js

We need to define the `alert` event handler in the actions object of the application route so that when the event bubbles up from the controller to the route, it will be handled in the route.

In the `alert` event handler, we set the `className` property of the application controller to `alert` so that it becomes visible from hidden. We also set the message that we passed through the `{{action}}` helper on the controller.

The `Ember.run.later` method is an Ember.js equivalent of the `setTimeout` method. It respects the Ember.js Run Loop. We will talk more about Ember.js Run Loop in the upcoming chapters.

Now you should be able to understand from the code that we show the alert for 2 seconds, and after that we set the CSS class of the alert to `hide`, which will hide the alert `<div>` element from the web page.

The effect of doing this is that when you click on the heading **Company Information Brochure**, you should see an alert on the top of the page that disappears after 2 seconds, as shown in the following screenshot:

Something went wrong from the Application Template

Company Information Brochure

Company Name	Headquarters	revenue
Google	Mountain View, California, United States of America	59825000000
Facebook	Menlo Park, California,United States of America	7870000000
twitter	San Francisco, California, United States of America	664000000

Application-wide alert box

Till now, we have created an alert that gets triggered on the click of a heading tag that is present in the application template. Normally, alerts like these will be triggered after performing some business logic that results in an error. This business logic can be placed in the `alert` event handler of the application.

Next, we would want to utilize the event bubbling capability of the framework to trigger this action from anywhere in the application. Let's change the index template to now trigger the `alert` action when anyone clicks on the different columns of the table, as shown in the following:

```
<table id="t01">
  <tr>
    <th>Company Name</th>
    <th>Headquarters</th>
    <th>revenue</th>
  </tr>
  {{#each item in model}}
  <tr>
    <td {{action "alert" "alert form company name"
      }}>{{item.name}}</td>
    <td {{action "alert" "alert form company headquarters"
      }}>{{item.headquarters}}</td>
    <td {{action "alert" "alert form revenue"
      }}>{{item.revenue}}</td>
  </tr>
  {{/each}}
</table>
```

The index template of chapter-5/example5 is present at chapter-5/example5/app/templates/index.hbs

As you can see, the template remains the same, with just one exception. We have now added the {{action}} helper in the <td> tag of the table. With our design, we now have the ability to pass in different messages from different parts of the application. This results in `alert` event being triggered on the click of different columns of the table. Doing this has enabled us to trigger application alert throughout the application in a consistent way.

What if we want to handle the events trigger by the index template in a different way? For this, we just need to define the index controller and write our business logic in the `alert` event handler of the controller, as shown in the following:

```
import Ember from 'ember';

export default Ember.ObjectController.extend({
  actions:{
    alert: function(){
      //do some controller level processing
      return true;
    }
  }
});
```

The index controller of chapter-5/example5 is present at chapter-5/example5/app/templates/index.js

Now, when we click on any of the columns of the table present in the index template, we can perform some logic there that is very specific to the index controller.

One very important thing to note here is the return true; statement at the end of the alert function. If the event handler returns true, it tells the framework to continue with the event bubbling and the event continues its propagation till the application route. If the alert event handler returns false, this would stop the event propagation and should be used in scenarios where different sections of the page have different alerts requirements.

Till now, all of our events got triggered on the mouse click. If you want to change this, you can use the on attribute of the actions helper to trigger the event on mouse up or mouse down, or so on:

```
{{action "alert" "message" on="mouseUp"}}
```

Handlebars.js input helpers

Ember.js provides us with some useful input helpers to manage text boxes, text areas, checkboxes, and select box.

You could do something like the following:

```
{{input type="text" value=firstName disabled=nameDisabled
  size="40"}}
```

This will render an HTML input box, whose value is bound to the firstName property in the controller. Similarly, the disabled property of the text box is bound to the nameDisabled property of the corresponding controller:

```
<div>Hi Mr. {{firstName}} {{lastName}}</div><br>
<div> Last Name is disabled: {{nameDisabled}}<br></div>
<br>
<div>First Name : {{input value=firstName size=20 }}</div>
<div> Last Name : {{input value=lastName
  disabled=nameDisabled}}</div>
<br><br>
<div>Enable last name ? {{input type="checkbox"
  checked=nameDisabled}}</div>
```

The index template of chapter-3/example6 is present at chapter-3/example6/app/templates/index.hbs

```
import Ember from 'ember';

export default Ember.ObjectController.extend({
  firstName: "",
  lastName: "Puri",
  nameDisabled: true
});
```

The index controller of chapter-3/example6 is present at chapter-3/example6/app/controller/index.js

In the preceding example, we have two input types: a text box to accept the first name and the last name, and a checkbox to enable/disable the last name textbox.

You can see in the previous example that the checked attribute of the checkbox and the disabled attribute of last name input box are bound to the same controller property `disableName`, which is by default set to true. Doing this would enable or disable the last name text box on checking, unchecking the `disable last name?` check box.

Similar to the text box, the text area input helper is self-explanatory and renders an HTML text area:

```
{{textarea value=longText cols="50" rows="4"}}
```

This would render a text area, whose value is bound to the `longText` property of the controller and has 50 columns and 4 rows.

Building custom Handlebars.js helpers

As seen in the earlier sections, Ember.js provides us with helper methods that enable us to do most common tasks very easily and quickly. But very soon we will end up in situations wherein we start duplicating tasks that were not possible with the default helpers. For example, we want to truncate text to be shown on the page to, say, 10 characters. One way to go about solving this problem would be to add a computed property in our controller, which binds to the long text property and returns the truncated text. This solution is not reusable as it is limited to one controller.

What if we could create our own helper tags that could be used application wide? The Ember.js framework lets you do that very easily. Let's see that by creating a custom truncate helper that will truncate the text passed to it, we would also need to pass in the length after which we truncate the text.

Helpers in Ember CLI projects go inside the `app/helpers` directory. The following truncate helper will go inside `app/helpers/truncate.js`:

```
import Ember from "ember";

export default function(value, options) {
  var length = 40;
  if(!Ember.isEmpty(options.hash.length)){
    length = options.hash.length;
  }
  if(!Ember.isEmpty(value)){
    if(value.length < length) {
      return value;
    }
    return value.substring(0, length) + "...";
  }
  return "";
};
```

The truncate helper is present at chapter-3/example7/app/helpers/truncate.js

You can see from the preceding code that we have defined a function that takes in a `value` and `options` arguments to handle the `truncate` helper. The helper method will truncate the text and will also respect any `length` attribute that is passed as an argument to the helper.

Ember CLI has two formats of writing the helper; these formats depend on the name of the helper method. Ember CLI encourages the helper names to contain a -. This helps disambiguate properties from helpers and improves the resolution performance of the framework as it is confident that the names containing - will be helpers. If the name of the helper contains a -, then the helper is resolved and will be registered automatically.

So, the above helper could be written as follows:

```
// app/helpers/trun-cate.js
import Ember from "ember";

export default Ember.Handlebars.makeBoundHelper(function(value,
  options) {
  // The same logic goes in here
});
```

Please note that if the name contains -, we export `Ember.Handlebars.makeBoundHelper`, instead of just the function. Doing this makes and registers the helper in Ember.js in one go.

When the name of the helper does not contain -, we will have to explicitly register the helper in `app/app.js` using `Ember.Handlebars.registerBoundHelper`.

```
import truncateHelper from './helpers/truncate';
Ember.Handlebars.registerBoundHelper('truncate', truncateHelper);
```

Here, as you can see, we are using the framework's `Ember.Handlebars.registerBoundHelper` to register our helper method. `Ember.Handlebars.registerBoundHelper` takes in two arguments: the helper name and a function that will be called when the helper is used.

Now let's see how we can use the helper method that we registered with our application:

```
{{truncate "This is very very long and beyond" length=20}}
<br>
{{truncate "this is very long" length=10}}
```

The truncate method being used in the index template is present at chapter-3/example7/app/templates/index.hbs

```
<h2>{{truncate "Welcome to Ember.js" length=10}}</h2>
{{outlet}}
```

The truncate helper being used in the application template is present at chapter-3/example7/app/templates/application.hbs

You can see that we can use our truncate Handlebars.js helper across the application, like any other helper method. We can also pass in the length attribute to make it more flexible.

If you run the above `chapter-3/example7` using `ember serve` and navigate to `http://locahost:4200`, you will see the truncated text, as shown in the following:

Using our truncate helper to truncate the text entered in the text box

Like our `truncate` helper, you can create other helpers to follow a set of style guidelines across your application. The benefit of this approach is very open-ended and depends on your imagination to bring consistency across your application.

Using the concise Emblem.js templating language

For some users, Handlebars.js may appear to be a very verbose template language as it uses plain HTML whereas users would prefer to use a more concise indentation-based language, something similar to Slim, Jade, Haml, and so on.

Thanks go to Alex Matchneer for creating Emblem.js, which is an indentation-based templating library like Slim, Jade, and Haml. So, if you have worked on any of these libraries before, you should be able to catch up with Emblem.js pretty quickly.

Emblem.js compiles to Handlebars.js and is fully compatible with the built-in Handlebars.js helpers that we have discussed in this chapter.

Installation

To use Emblem.js, you need to run the following command in your Ember application directory, which in our case is `chapter-3/example8/`:

```
ember install:addon ember-cli-emblem-hbs-printer
emberinstall:npm emblem
```

This will install the add-on emblem compiler that is compatible with the Ember CLI asset pipeline. More information about the Ember emblem add-on can be found at: `https://github.com/201-created/ember-cli-emblem-hbs-printer`.

Using Emblem.js

Creating an Emblem.js template is very similar to what we have been doing till now with Handlebars.js, except for the change in the extension of the file. The template files now end with `.embl` or `.emblem`, instead of `.hbs`:

```
h2 Welcome to Ember.js Application, it uses Emblem.js,
   the concise indentation based templating library
   = outlet
```

The application emblem template is present at chapter-3/example8/app/templates/application.emblem

```
h3 From Index Template
  ul
    each item in model
    li=item
```

The index emblem template is present at chapter-3/example8/app/templates/index.emblem

You can see in the above that instead of using plain HTML, we use a different syntax, which is based on indentation. All the elements are rendered based on how you arrange different elements of your template via spaces.

You can see that `h3` and the `ul` tag are at the same level. Similarly, the `each` loop is nested inside the `ul` tag. The `li` tag is nested within the `each` loop block. We use two spaces to nest an element inside its parent element.

The benefit of indentation-based templates is that they are very concise and readable, as you don't have to search for closing HTML tags as you do in plain HTML.

This section gives you a very brief introduction to Emblem.js. We will not be covering the syntax and detailed working of Emblem.js in this book, and it is left to the reader to refer to `http://emblemjs.com/` and `https://github.com/machty/emblem.js` for more information about the framework.

Summary

In this chapter, you learned in detail about the Ember.js template library, Handlebars.js. We saw how effectively Handlebars.js template library solves the most common templating issues of today's ambitious web applications.

You learned how the design choices made by Handlebars.js make your Ember.js application extensible and easy to understand. You looked at different Handlebars.js expressions, conditionals, and iterators. You saw how effective the Handlebars.js helper methods are in helping us build complex templates. Then, you learned how easy it is to create your own helpers. The extensibility of the frameworks speaks for itself when we are able to plug a new templating library Emblem.js, instead of Handlebars.js.

In the next chapter, you will learn about one of the most important parts of the Ember.js application, the router. You will learn how to maintain state in our application using the router.

4
Managing Application State Using Ember.js Routes

In the last chapter, we learned about the Ember.js template layer. We learned how to use the Ember.js template markup, expression, and helpers to create complex templates. In this chapter, we will focus on the Ember.js routes. We will see how to manage your application state, using the Ember.js router.

In this chapter, we will cover the following topics:

- Application state
- Creating your first route
- Resources and nested templates
- Injecting the model for your template
- Making routes dynamic
- Setting up the controller
- Customizing templates to render
- The location API

Application state

URL, or Uniform Resource Locator, is one of the most important parts of any web application. With time, URLs have evolved from just referring a static resource on the server to identifying and managing the complete state of modern web applications.

State, as defined by FOLDOC (`http://foldoc.org/state`), is how something is — its configuration, attributes, condition, or information content. An application state is created when the user first requests the URL for the web application. As the user interacts with the application, the state of web application changes.

In Ember.js, the URL represents each of the possible states in your application. It can be thought as the serialization of application current state. As the user interacts with the application, the URL governs what the user is presented on screen. This means that there is a direct mapping between the URL and the state of the application. The router in Ember.js is responsible for maintaining this mapping.

When an Ember.js application first loads up, the router is responsible for setting up application state that corresponds to the current URL. The application state for an Ember.js application involves loading data for a specific route, setting up the model and controller, displaying the handlebars template corresponding to the route, and more.

Creating your first route

Till now most of our examples in our previous chapters have been using the `index` or `/` route. Real-world web applications seldom have only one route. Ambitious web applications, on the other hand, have a separate URL endpoint mapped to each different state of the application.

The Ember.js framework provides the concept of a router, a route, and a resource to manage the mapping between the URL and the state of the application.

Router in Ember.js is the core and the central part of the framework. It maintains the mapping of the URLs to individual routes. It monitors the URL of the web application and then, based on the mapping, it invokes the individual routes.

Let's see how to add this mapping. We will be adding two new routes, `products` and `about`, to our application.

The `Router` definition present at `example1/app/router.js` is as follows:

```
import Ember from 'ember';
import config from './config/environment';

var Router = Ember.Router.extend({
  location: config.locationType // "auto"
});

Router.map(function() {
  this.route("products",{ path: "/products" });
```

```
    this.route("about",{ path: "/about" });
});
```

```
export default Router;
```

As you can see, we first create the `Router` object by extending `Ember.Router`. The `location` property of the router governs how to build the URLs of the application. We will be talking about the location API later in this chapter.

We use the `map` method of `Ember.Router` to create individual routes. We use the `this.route` method of the router to map URLs with the routes. The `route` method takes in three arguments: `name`, `options`, and `callback`.

The `name` corresponds to the name of the route and helps in identifying this route from other parts of the application.

The `options` argument expects a JavaScript object with your desired options set. In our case, we pass in the `path` attribute in the option's argument object to map our route to a specific URL.

The last argument is the `callback`, which is used for nesting the routes.

As you can see in the preceding code, we defined two routes with names `products` and `about`.

> Please note here that if you want to keep the name of the route and of the URL pattern same, you can omit the additional path property, which is set in the `options` object. So `this.route("products",{ path: "/products" });` and `this.route("products")` will essentially mean the same thing.

Let's now look at the templates for these corresponding routes. As discussed in the previous chapter, all the templates go inside the `app/templates/` folder.

```
<h2>Welcome to Ember.js</h2>
<div> {{#link-to 'about'}}About{{/link-to}} </div>
<div> {{#link-to 'products'}}Products{{/link-to}}</div>
{{outlet}}
```

The application template is present at example1/app/templates/application.hbs

```
<br>
<br>
<div>Products Template</div>
```

The products template is present at example1/app/templates/products.hbs

```
<br>
<br>
<div>About Template</div>
```

The products template is present at example1/app/templates/about.hbs

You can see from what precedes that apart from the application template, we have defined two additional templates, `products` and `about`. These templates contain the data to be displayed for the `products` and `about` pages.

In `application.hbs`, we are also using a very useful handlebars helper expression, `{{#link-to}}`. The `link-to` helper expression helps us avoid hardcoding the URL address in our application. It fetches the URL pattern from the mappings in the router.

So `{{#link-to 'products'}} Products {{/link-to}}` would generate something like the following:

```
<a id="ember258" class="ember-view" href="/about">About</a>.
```

You can see that the generated HTML link's `href` points to the correct URL path. The `link-to` helper makes our application transparent to any changes in the URL pattern of the application.

Let us say that later in development cycle of your application, the **SEO** (**search engine optimization**) expert comes in and suggests that by changing the `/about` endpoint to `/about-us`, you will improve the search engine ranking for your site.

If you had used the `{{link-to}}` helper, you would just edit the router code to map to `about-us` instead of `about`, and your application would work just fine. Had you hardcoded the URL in your application, incorporating this change would have been error-prone and time consuming.

If you run the above code, you will see a screen that now has `About` and `Products` links on the homepage.

If you click on any of the links, you will see that the respective `products` or `about` template appears on the screen, as shown in the following figure:

Welcome to Ember.js

About
Products

Products Template

The products template rendered when a user clicks on the products link

In Ember.js, the routes of your application should inherit the framework's `Ember.Route` class to provide any custom implementation of the route. One thing that you might have noticed in the preceding example would be that we did not create `app/routes/products.js` or `app/routes/about.js` in our application. Whenever a user visits the `/products` or `/about` URL, the Ember.js framework tries to find the corresponding routes based on naming conventions. For example, for `/products`, the router will try and instantiate `app/routes/products.js` for you, and if the framework is not able to find its definition, then it will generate the route for you. So, in our case, since we don't define the `app/routes/products.js` or `app/routes/about.js`, the Ember.js framework generates them for us. Ember.js frameworks rely heavily on naming conventions, and routes are at the core of these conventions. Based on the name of the route supplied to the `this.route()` function, the framework tries to find the respective controller and template to use.

Let's see this by an example; in the above example, we created the product route which uses the following:

```
this.route("products",{ path: "/products" });
```

When the end user visits the `/products` path, the framework will try to find the route with the matching name and path, and will look for definition exported in `app/routes/products.js`, and when it finds one, it will instantiate the route for you and execute the hooks associated with the route (we will be covering the initialization of routes in more detail later in this chapter).

Then, the framework will try to find the controller that matches the route, which in our case should be defined in the `app/controllers/products.js` file. The framework will finally resolve the handlebars.js template it has to render, which should be defined in the `app/templates/products.hbs` file.

As you can see, this clearly forms a pattern. An `example` route declaration will map to the `/example` URL by default, and the framework will look for its matching route definition exported from the `app/routes/example.js` file, matching controller in `app/controllers/example.js`, and render the template defined in `app/templates/example.hbs`.

Now, since all of the application will follow this convention, it becomes really easy to find where the code for a specific functionality resides. It also makes debugging errors in your application very straightforward.

Resources and nested templates

Till now, we have seen very basic usage of the Ember.js routes; we have been using only top-level routes such as /products and /about, but very seldom do real-world applications have such simple routes.

Real-world applications will have resources or nouns, and actions that can be executed on these nouns that are depicted by verbs.

For example, there could be a /products/2 endpoint to show the product details page for a product with ID as 2, or /products/new and /products/2/edit routes to create and edit a product, respectively.

The Ember.js framework encourages using resource for all the nouns and route for all the verbs. This means that if you are creating your application for a specific domain area, all the entities of that domain should map to a resource and all the actions on the domain entities should translate to routes. A resource then becomes a collection of routes.

You can create a new resource using this.resource in the router. It expects two arguments, the first one is the name of the resource and other is a function that defines the nested routes, if any. If you don't have any nested routes in the resource, you can omit this argument. The following code snippet shows how to create a resource with nested routes:

```
Router.map(function() {
  this.resource("products",function(){
    this.route("new");
  });
  this.route("about");
});
```

The nested route is defined in example2/app/router.js

Here, we have created a resource products and a nested route, new. To be able to display these routes, we will have to create the corresponding nested templates.

One very important thing to note here is that the nesting of resources/routes also means that their templates should also be nested in a similar fashion. Let's make it more clearer by defining our products , products/new and about templates:

```
<br>
<br>
<div>Products Template</div>
    {{outlet}}
```

The products template is present at example2/app/templates/products.hbs

```
<br>
<br>
<div>About Template</div>
<div> This Template should contains some information about us
```

The about template is present at example2/app/templates/about.hbs

```
<br>
<h3>Create a New Product</h3>
<br>
    Product name:<br>
    {{input value=name }}
<br>
    Product Description:<br>
    {{textarea value=description }}
<br><br>
<button {{action 'create'}}>Create</button>
```

The products.new template is present at example2/app/templates/products/new.hbs

You can see above that we have defined two templates, one for `products` and the other for the `new` route that is nested under the `products` resource.

When you first look at the `products` template, you will notice that we have now added `{{outlet}}` at the end of the template. This outlet will enable nesting for this template, and all the nested routes that are present under the `products` resource will first render the `products` template present at `app/templates/products.hbs`, and then render the nested route's template in the outlet provided by the `products` template. If you remove the `{{outlet}}` from the `products` template, you will notice that the `products.new` template is never rendered, as it could not get the parent outlet to render the child route template.

You might also have noticed by now that we are referring to the `new` route that is nested inside the `products` resource by `products.new`. Ember.js follows this convention to refer to the nested routes in handlebars and other helpers, which is `<<parent resource>>.<<nested route>>`.

To link this nested route using the `{{link-to}}` handlebars helper, we would do something like the following:

```
{{#link-to 'products.new'}}Create a new product{{/link-to}}</div>
```

The following table shows the mapping of the different routes that you defined in your router to respective controller, route, and template files:

URL	Route name	Controller	Route	Template
/	index	app/ controllers/ index.js	app/routes/ index.js	app/ templates/ index.hbs
N/A	products	app/ controllers/ products.js	app/routes/ products.js	app/ templates/ products.hbs
/products	products. index	app/ controllers/ products.js ↳ app/ controllers/ products/ index.js	app/routes/ products.js ↳ app/routes/ products/ index.js	app/ templates/ products.hbs ↳app/ templates/ products/ index.hbs
/products/ new	products. new	app/ controllers/ products.js ↳ app/ controllers/ products/new. js	app/routes/ products.js ↳ app/routes/ products/ new.js	app/ templates/ products.hbs ↳ app/ templates/ products/new. hbs
/about	about	app/ controllers/ about.js	app/routes/ about.js	app/ templates/ about.hbs

Let us see how the routes, which we have defined in our router above, map and initialize the controller, route, and template. Let us start from products.new route. Now, since the new route is defined inside the products resource, we would refer it by products.new. As we discussed earlier, route nesting also means controller and template nesting. This means that when the user visits the /products/new route, first of all, the products template is rendered from app/templates/products.hbs using the route exported from app/routes/products.js, and this route injects the controller from app/controllers/products.js to back the template.

After rendering the products template, the framework will look for the products. new template in app/template/products/new.hbs to render it in the {{outlet}} provided by the products template.

The controller exported at `app/controllers/products/new.js` and the route exported at `app/routes/products/new.js` will back the `app/templates/products/new.hbs` template.

The general rule of thumb is that first the parent resource is rendered, using its route and controller. Then, the nested child route is rendered in the parent template's outlet.

The nested or child route has its own controller and route, just like an independent route. The location of the nested route should be inside a folder whose name is the name of the resource it is nested in, for example, `app/routes/<<resource>>/<<nested route>>`.

It may seem a bit odd at first, but the trick here is to think of your application layout as nested templates rather than independent ones.

One thing that you might have noticed in the above table would be the `products` route, which is not mapped to any URL, and the `products.index` route, which we did not define anywhere. Lets revisit the `products` and `products.index` routes again here:

URL	Route name	Controller	Route	Template
N/A	products	`app/controllers/products.js`	`app/routes/products.js`	`app/templates/products.hbs`
/products	products.index	`app/controllers/products.js` ↳`app/controllers/products/index.js`	`app/routes/products.js` ↳`app/routes/products/index.js`	`app/templates/products.hbs` ↳`app/templates/products/index.hbs`

The `products` route is not mapped to any URL and is always invoked when a user visits `/products` or any of its child routes. It is very much like the application route present in `app/routes/application.js`, but only for all the routes that are nested inside the `products` resource.

If we want to handle errors or add in a common functionality for all the products, then its `app/routes/products.js` or `app/controllers/products.js` routes would be the right place to put in the common behavior.

For example, if we want to handle the errors that originate from the products pages in a specific way, we would put this specific behavior in the `products` route.

Similarly, whenever you create a nested route, you get `resource.index` that maps to `/resource` automatically. You just need to override the default implementation of `ResourceIndexRoute` and `ResourceIndexController` by defining them in your application with its custom behavior. This behavior is in line with the event bubbling topic we discussed in *Action event bubbling* section of *Chapter 3, Rendering Using Templates*.

This hierarchy of controllers and routes keeps the entities focused toward providing functionality to one section, rather than putting everything in one place and later finding it difficult to maintain that. Another view of the template hierarchy of our application is shown in the following image:

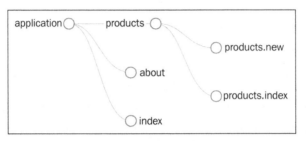

Template hierarchy of our application

Now, you should be in a better position to understand the overall routes and template nesting in Ember.js.

Injecting the model for your template

Till now, almost all of the examples we have seen so far have one thing in common: they all render static data that is returned from the `model` method of the corresponding route, something like the following:

```
export default Ember.Route.extend({
  model: function() {
    return ['red', 'yellow', 'blue'];
  }
});
```

As we saw in *Chapter 2, Understanding Ember.js Object-oriented Patterns*, one of the very important advantages of using Ember.js framework is that it tries to build an application that uses components that are highly decoupled, yet internally cohesive.

The templates present the data that is fetched from the models. Routes play a very important role in this process. Routes help you to decide which model to fetch and how to customize it. As shown in the preceding snippet, the model can return a static list of colors or it can also fetch a list of colors from a remote server. All of this remains transparent to the templates that focus on displaying the list of item(s) returned from the model method.

Up until now, we have seen the model method in the route returning static data to the templates. But it will seldom be the case where your models return static data, and most of the time the data is fetched from the server and displayed to the user.

For the next example, we will be using GitHub's public API (found at `https://developer.github.com/v3/`)to fetch the commits in the Ember.js repository.

If you open the `https://api.github.com/repos/emberjs/ember.js/commits` link in a browser, you will get the commit data in JSON format for the Ember.js repository on GitHub, something like the following:

```
[{
  "sha": "2da6e0b981ee20d2e2361102fcf7b8cb3ef812c5",
  "commit": {
    "author": {
      "name": "Stefan Penner",
      "email": "stefan.penner@gmail.com",
      "date": "2014-12-06T17:38:03Z"
    },
    "committer": {
      "name": "Stefan Penner",
      "email": "stefan.penner@gmail.com",
      "date": "2014-12-06T17:38:03Z"
    },
    "message": "Merge pull request #9826 from twokul/
      brocfile-dup-funct\n\nRemoves duplicate function",
    "tree": {
      "sha": "3eaae01753f4a2a919921232013ba32dda658bab",
      "url": "https://api.github.com/repos/emberjs/ember.js/git/
        trees/3eaae01753f4a2a919921232013ba32dda658bab"
    },
    "url": "https://api.github.com/repos/emberjs/ember.js/
      git/commits/2da6e0b981ee20d2e2361102fcf7b8cb3ef812c5",
    "comment_count": 0
  },
]
```

Now, let's consume this data and make it presentable for an end user.

We shall create two routes here: the `commits.index` route and the application `index` route.

As we don't have anything at present to show on the homepage of our application, we shall use the `redirect` method to transition from the `index` route to the `commits.index` route when anyone hits the / or the root URL. This is how the `commits.index` route will look:

```
export default  Ember.Route.extend({
  model: function() {
    varurl =
      'https://api.github.com/repos/emberjs/ember.js/commits';
    return Ember.$.getJSON(url);
  }
});
```

Commits index route is present at example3/app/routes/commits/index.js

The following code shows how we can redirect the index route of our application to `commits.index` route:

```
export default Ember.Route.extend({
  redirect: function(){
    this.transitionTo("commits.index");
  }
});
```

Application index route is present at example3/app/routes/index.js

As you can see in the preceding code snippet, we are using the `JQuery $.getJSON()` method to retrieve the data from the server. Now, instead of static text, our `model` function retrieves the commit data from the server and returns it to the template.

Now let's look at the two templates we will have for our application. One is for the application that will contain our application name. The application template can contain things that are common for the entire application. The other `commits.index` template can contain the code to display the list of commits of the repository. These commits can be retrieved from the model object set in the `commits.index` route, as shown in the following:

```
<h1>Ember.js Repo</h2>
{{outlet}}
```

Application template is present at example3/app/templates/application.hbs

```
<h2>Commits</h2>
{{#each c in model}}
<div><em>Sha</em>: {{c.sha}}</div>
<div><em>Author</em>: {{c.commit.author.name}}</div>
<div><em>Message</em>: {{c.commit.message}}</div>
<hr/>
{{/each}}
```

The commits.index template is present at example3/app/templates/commits/index.hbs

As you can see in the `example3/app/templates/commits/index.hbs` file, to show the list of commits, we just iterate over the model object and then just output the contents of each commit to the user. If you run the preceding code, you will see the output as shown in the following screenshot:

Using asynchronous data from the model

Making routes dynamic

Now we have successfully returned the data fetched from the server on the invocation of a route. Let's move ahead and see how can we make our routes dynamic. Till now, the URL that maps to our routes has been fixed. There may be situations in which we may want to read parts of URL and then act according to what was received. For example, we may want to make the `/products/:product_id` route, which shows the product page with ID equal to `:product_id`, or, like in our above example, we may want to create a new route `/commits/:sha` to display the information of a specific commit.

The above dynamism in Ember.js routes is achieved through **dynamic segments**. Dynamic segments in routes start with :. Let's see this by an example. We shall continue the above example and create a new screen to link to template that shows information about a specific commit.

Let's look at the JavaScript code. First, in the router, we need to define two routes—one for complete list of the commits and one for individual detail of a specific commit:

```
Router.map(function(){
  this.resource("commits",function(){
    this.route("commit",{path:":sha"});
  });
});
```

The application router is present at example3/app/router.js

This would result in a route hierarchy that is similar to the following figure:

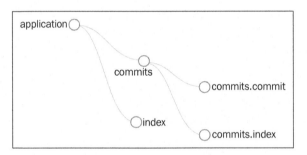

Route hierarchy of the GitHub commits application

You can see that at the top level is the application route. We get the index route for free, but we are not using that route in our application, as we would focus on the `commits` resource here.

Now, since we created `commits` as a resource, we would get `commits.index` route automatically by the framework, which would map to the `/commits/` URL.

The commit route created inside the `commits` resource is meant to show the details of a particular commit. As you can see in the router code, we have made this route dynamic by including the `:sha` dynamic segment into it:

```
this.route("commit",{path:":sha"});
```

Let us now look at the route's code:

```
import Ember from "ember";

export default Ember.Route.extend({
  model: function(params){
    console.log("model hook called");
    varurl =
      'https://api.github.com/repos/emberjs/ember.js/commits/'+
      params.sha;
    return Ember.$.getJSON(url);
  },
  serialize: function(model){
    return {sha: model.sha};
  }
});
```

The commits.commit dynamic route to get the information for a specific commit is
present at example3/app/routes/commits/commit.js

The `commits.commit` route fetches the details of a particular commit that is identified by a unique SHA and returns a model that contains the commit object.

This SHA makes our route dynamic and hence we would need to handle that in our routes. For that, we would need to get the dynamic segment from the `params` variable that is passed on to the `model` method.

```
varurl = 'https://api.github.com/repos/emberjs/ember.js/commits/'+
  params.sha;
```

You can see that we use `params.sha` to access the dynamic segment we defined in the route. Please note here that the name of the dynamic segment is the one that we defined in the router, such as the following:

```
this.route("commit",{path:":sha"});
```

We just need to omit the `:` to get the variable name. Let's make it more clearer by another example.

If you defined a route with dynamic route as follows:

```
this.route("product",{path:"/products/:category/:name"});
```

Here, we have defined two dynamic segments in the URL: `name` and `category`. We can access these dynamic segments in our route by using `params.category` and `params.name` variables, respectively.

Route's serialize method

Now, as we are using dynamic segment (`:sha`) in our `commits.commit` route whenever we programmatically call this route using the `{{#link-to}}` helper, we need a way to extract the URL `params` from the `model` object passed to the `{{#link-to}}` helper, so that the framework can construct the right URL for the application. The `serialize` method is used exactly that same purpose. This method takes in the model and returns the equivalent of the `params` object that can be used to generate the URLs of the given route. In our case, we would need to return an object that would have a `sha` property and its corresponding value.

In our template, you will see that we use the `{{#link-to}}` helper to link the SHA of a commit to its route:

```
{{#link-to 'commits.commit' c}}{{c.sha}}{{/link-to}}
```

When we use this `link-to` helper, it will use the `App.CommitsCommit` route's `serialize` method to build the dynamic URL.

If you don't return the required object from the `serialize` method, you would notice that the generated URL will be of the form `/commits/undefined`, which is not the expected behavior.

Setting up the controller

In all of the above examples, we assume that the model object that is returned from the model method of the corresponding route is automatically available in the templates. Here, we will look at how this automatic behavior is implemented in Ember.js, and if you want to change this behavior, how should you do it.

`Ember.Route` defines a hook that can be used to alter this default behavior. This hook is defined in the `setupController` method. The default implementation of `setupController` sets the `model` property of the controller. This `model` property is fetched from the `model` method in the corresponding route definition:

```
setupController: function(controller, model) {
  controller.set('model', model);
}
```

The default implementation of route's setupController function

So, if you want to set a different property than `model` on the controller to be accessible by the templates, you will have to change that behavior by providing your own implementation of the `setupController` method in your route.

There are times when you would want to add or set additional properties on the controller that maps to the route. All the additional properties changes should go in your route's `setupController` function:

```
setupController: function(controller, model) {
  this._super(controller,model);
  controller.set("myProperty","myValue");
}
```

You can see that we set an additional property on the controller here using `controller.set`.

One thing you need to be sure of is that when you provide your own implementation of `setupController`, the default behavior will not be executed. To keep the default behavior of setting the model property on the controller, you should call the `this._super` method, which will execute the `Ember.RoutersetupController` function and will keep the default behavior intact.

Customizing templates to render

Up until now, we have seen that when you visit a URL `/example`, which maps to route `app/routes/example.js` and `app/routes/example/index.js`, this renders `app/templates/example.hbs` and `app/templates/example/index.hbs` templates. To change this behavior, Ember.js provides us with a hook that is used to resolve which templates to render for the current route.

One common use case for customizing which templates to render is when your application template has multiple outlets and you want to render a particular route on an outlet other than the default one.

Let's see this by an example. We will be using the `bootstrap` library in our project. For this, we need to first install the `bootstrap` dependency in our project by using the following:

bower install --save-dev bootstrap

So, in the `chapter-4/example4` directory, we need to run the preceding command. This should fetch and install the `bootstrap` library in the `example4/bower-components/` directory. Now we need to tell our asset pipeline broccoli to include the bootstrap assets (css, js, fonts, images) in our `vendor.js` and `vendor.css` files. To do this, we will have to make changes in `example4/app/Brocfile.js`, and we will have to add the following lines in the file:

```
app.import('bower_components/bootstrap/dist/css/bootstrap.css');
app.import('bower_components/bootstrap/dist/css/
  bootstrap.css.map', { destDir: 'assets' });
app.import('bower_components/bootstrap/dist/fonts/
  glyphicons-halflings-regular.eot', { destDir: 'fonts' });
app.import('bower_components/bootstrap/dist/fonts/
  glyphicons-halflings-regular.ttf', { destDir: 'fonts' });
app.import('bower_components/bootstrap/dist/fonts/
  glyphicons-halflings-regular.svg', { destDir: 'fonts' });
app.import('bower_components/bootstrap/dist/fonts/
  glyphicons-halflings-regular.woff', { destDir: 'fonts' });
app.import('bower_components/bootstrap/dist/js/bootstrap.js');
```

The bootstrap-specific files which we need to add to Brocfile.js

Now, we are good to go and we can now start using the bootstrap glyph icons, css, and js in our code.

We will consider a use case in which our application has a sidebar and a main body content. Both the sidebar and the main body should be customizable. This also means that our different routes can have different sidebars and body content.

The code for this example is present at `https://github.com/suchitpuri/emberjs-essentials/tree/master/chapter-4/example4`.

Since our application has a sidebar and a main body, let us first create the application template that accommodates these two components. Since these components are customizable, we will have to define two outlets to render route-specific content in these two components.

If you look at `application.hbs`, present at `example4/app/templates/application.hbs`, you will notice that we have defined two templates: one for the sidebar content and one for the body:

```
<ul class="sidebar-nav" id="sidebar">
  {{outlet sidebar}}
</ul>
<div class="row">
  <div class="col-md-12">
    {{outlet}}
```

```
    </div>
  </div>
```

Code snippet from application.hbs is present at example4/app/templates/application.hbs

Now, we need to tell our routes to render different templates in different outlets. Ember.js provides us with a hook to override which template to render in different outlets.

The `renderTemplate` method of `Ember.Route` provides this hook. The default behavior of this hook is to render the matching template in the `application` outlet of its parent route.

Now, as our requirement is different, we will have to override this method to provide our implementation of rendering the template matching this route.

Let's look at the `index` route of our application, as follows:

```
import Ember from "ember";
export default Ember.Route.extend({
  renderTemplate: function(){
    this.render('sidebar',{
      outlet: "sidebar"
    });
    this.render('index')
  }
});
```

The index route is present at example4/app/routes/index.js

In the preceding code, we use `this.render` method to tell the router about the name and options of the template to render. The first argument is the name of the template to render. The options object can supply the following properties:

```
{
into: 'favoritePost',// the template to render into
outlet: 'comment',// The name of the outlet in that template
controller: 'blogPost'//The controller to use for that template
}
```

The `into` property specifies which template to render the current template in, the `outlet` property specifies which outlet to use in the above template, and the `controller` property specifies which controller to use when rendering the specified template.

As you can see from the above index route code, when anyone visits the / URL, we inform the index route to render the sidebar template in the sidebar outlet and the index template in the default application template.

Similarly, we can create other additional routes that render different templates inside their respective outlets. For example, in our example4 application, we define another route named as about, which renders the about_sidebar template in the sidebar outlet, and the about template in the default unnamed outlet present in the about template.

```
import Ember from "ember";
export default Ember.Route.extend({
renderTemplate: function(){
this.render('about_sidebar',{
outlet: "sidebar"
    });
this.render('about')
  }
});
```

The about route is present in example4/app/routes/about.js

When you run this application and open http://localhost:4200/ on your browser, you will see something like the following screenshot:

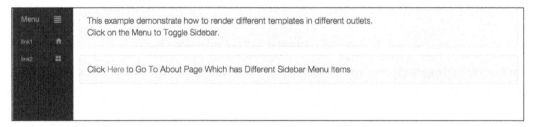

The running application with sidebar

Now, when you navigate to the http://localhost:4200/about, you will see that both the sidebar and the page content change, as shown in the following screenshot:

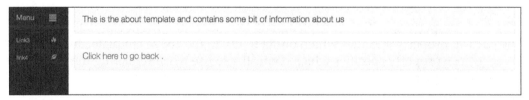

Different sidebar and body content being rendered when you visit the about route in your application

The location API

At the start of this chapter, when we were discussing about the `router.js`, or the application router that manages different URL states of the application, we passed in the location property to our `Router` object. The property was being read from `config/environment.js` file:

```
var Router = Ember.Router.extend({
  location: config.locationType
});
```

The Router definition is present at example1/app/router.js

If you look into the `config/environment.js` file, you will see that the location property is set to `auto` for development and production environments and for test environments it is set to `none`.

The location API governs how to generate URLs for your application. The `location` property can be assigned one of these four values: `hash`, `history`, `auto`, and `none`.

If you set the location property of your router to `hash`, then the generated URLs of your application will have a # in them and will be of the form `/#/route`. This type of location tracking depends on the `hashchange` event existing in the browser to detect any changes in the URL.

The `history` location type is more recent and is available in latest browsers (IE 10+, Firefox 31+, Chrome 31+) only. This will result in URLs that are similar to the normal URLs, that is, without the #. This technique uses the browser's history API to keep track of URL changes. The resulting URLs will be of the form `/route`.

The auto-location type decides on which type to use, based on the browser. If the browser supports the history API, the application will use `history` as the location type, otherwise it will fall back to `hash` location type.

The last location type available is `none`. If you set your router's location type to `none`, then your router will not store the application URL state in the URL and the URL will remain constant throughout the application. This type of location is generally used for testing purposes.

Summary

In this chapter, you learned about navigating to different states of your application using Ember.Router. You saw how to create our own routes and resources. You learned how to use dynamic segments in your routes, thereby making your routes read properties from the URL. Then, you learned about how to create nested routes and the naming conventions associated with it. You looked at how easy it is to customize the route's behavior to set or change properties on the controller backing the template. Then, you learned about how you can render templates into different outlets of our application. Finally, you looked at what location API means and what the four different types of values that can be assigned to the location property of our router are.

In the next chapter, you will learn about how to effectively communicate with the API server using Ember Data.

5
Handling Display Logic Using Ember.js Controllers

In the last chapter, you learned about the Ember.js routing layer. You learned how to manage your application state by using Ember.js router and routes. In this chapter, you will learn about the Ember.js controllers. You will see how to decorate your models with view-specific logic, using Ember.js controllers.

In this chapter, we shall cover the following topics:

- Introducing controllers
- Object controllers and array controllers
- Connecting controllers

Introducing controllers

Like all the other components in the Ember.js framework, the controllers are also well-designed thought of components. Controllers in Ember.js are designed to serve the following three main use cases:

- **Handle user interaction**: As discussed in *Chapter 3, Rendering Using Templates*, under the *Action event bubbling* section, all user actions and events are first made available to the controller associated with the template and then are bubbled up to the route hierarchy. This makes controllers an ideal place to handle all the action and events that deal with the UI of the application. For example, many times you would want to show/hide/collapse elements on the page, based on certain user interactions. Such actions and events should be handled in the controller.

- **Make models available to templates**: Templates don't have direct knowledge or access to the models related to a specific route. Models are made available to the template via controllers. The corresponding `Route` sets the model property on the controller that can be easily accessed by the template.

- **Maintaining nonpersistent state**: Sometimes you need to work with data that doesn't have anything to do with your models. A good example would be to store the current filter that the user has selected in a product search. Such properties can be stored very easily on the controller.

Overall, controllers in the Ember.js framework should work on things that your application does not need to save to the server.

Templates in Ember.js framework only talk directly to the controllers (refer to the following image). This means that it is the responsibility of the controller to present the template with all the data it needs:

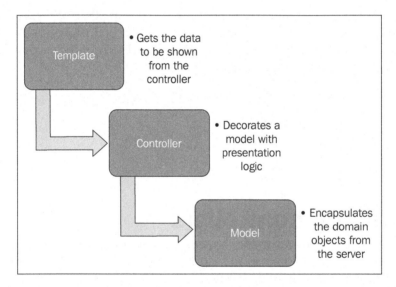

In almost all of the examples we have seen so far, we were setting up the model property in the `Route` object. This `model` property is automatically set on the corresponding controller and is made available to the templates.

To make this even more seamless, controllers in Ember.js act like a proxy for model properties. This enables you to use `{{property}}` instead of `{{model.property}}` in your templates. The properties that are used in templates are first looked up in the controller; if it's found, it is served to the templates, and if it's not found, it is then looked up in the model property of the controller.

Controllers in Ember.js also decorate the models that are fetched from the server. Sometimes, it may happen that we are storing the information in a specific way and want to present the information to the user in a different way.

To solve this particular problem, you could transform the data either on the server side (API) or on the client side (Ember.js application).

Transforming the data on the server side means that the server now needs to understand how this information is consumed by a web application in order for the communication to work properly.

Transforming the data on the client side means that the server can remain indifferent to the consumers of the API and leave it to the clients to transform the data, according to their needs.

The drawback of the first approach is that the server becomes very tightly coupled with the web application .If tomorrow you decide to build a mobile application that uses the same API but needs the to present data in a different way, you will have to either make a new API or change the existing API by adding transformations for the new client. This approach is not scalable and can become unmanageable when there are too many clients consuming your API.

The second approach, on the other hand, works very well with any number of clients, as it is left to the clients to transform the data received from the server. To implement this, the application must transform the data received, and the design of transformations must be extensible and scalable so that the application is able to transform the data received, irrespective of the communication protocol.

When we use a framework like Ember.js, we get the capabilities with well-designed components discussed previously as part of the second approach. Apart from controllers in which you can add computed properties that transform the data received from the server, Ember.js also provides us with data transformers that are specially designed to transform the data received from the server as part of the `ember-data` library.

Object controller and array controller

Ember.js provides us with two types of controllers: `Ember.ObjectController` and `Ember.ArrayController`. We have been using `Ember.ObjectController` in many examples throughout this book. `ObjectController` works on one object and `ArrayController` works on an array or list of objects.

When we say that `ObjectController` works on a single object, we mean that the model property of the corresponding route returns the single JavaScript object and not an array. You can also use the `setupController` hook that was discussed in the previous chapter to set the model property of the controller. The default behavior of the `setupController` method is to set the model property on the controller to what is returned from the model method present in the route. So, you can either set the model in `setupController` or return the object from the model method present in the route.

`ArrayController`, on the other hand, has been designed to work on a list of items and hence the model, or the `setupController` hook, should set the model to an array of objects.

Let's see how can we use the `ArrayController` to display a list of products that is received from the server or similar.

The first thing we would need to do is to return an array of products from the model property of our corresponding route. Here, in our example, we will be using the products route to show the list of products:

```
import Ember from "ember";

export default Ember.Route.extend({
  model: function(){
    return[
      {
        "name":"Leather Jacket",
        "description":"A very long jacket description which cannot
          be shown inside a table and will have to be shortened",
        "currency":"USD",
        "symbol":"$",
        "price":"1999.999",
        "dimensions":{
          "length":7.0,
          "width":12.0,
          "height":9.5
        }
      },
      {
        "name":"Some Coat",
        "description":"A very long coat description which cannot
          be shown inside a table and will have to be shortened",
        "currency":"EURO",
        "symbol":"€",
        "price":"299.999",
        "dimensions":{
```

```
                "length":8.0,
                "width":11.0,
                "height":10.0
            }
        },
        {
            "name":"T Shirt",
            "description":"A very long T Shirt description which
                cannot be shown inside a table and will have to be
                shortened",
            "currency":"USD",
            "symbol":"$",
            "price":"58.999",
            "dimensions":{
                "length":9.0,
                "width":13.0,
                "height":11.0
            }
        },
        {
            "name":"White Shirt",
            "description":"A very long Shirt description which cannot
                be shown inside a table and will have to be shortened",
            "currency":"GBP",
            "symbol":"£",
            "price":"1999.9999",
            "dimensions":{
                "length":10.0,
                "width":14.0,
                "height":12.0
            }
        }
    ]
  }
});
```

The products route is present at app/routes/products.js

Here, we returned a static list of products from the `model` property of our route, but in most real-world cases, this would be fetched from the backend server. Here, each of our products has a `name`, `description`, `currency`, `symbol`, `price`, and `dimensions` property. The only issue is that the `price` is a floating point number and not a formatted number, so we will have to format the price and show it properly with the currency symbol. Also, the description that comes from the backend server is too long to be displayed in a table, so we will have to truncate that, as well.

Since most of the changes discussed above are related to the UI of the table, putting the functionality in the `controller` seems an obvious choice.

Let's look at the `products` controller:

```
import Ember from "ember";

export default Ember.ArrayController.extend({
  sortProperties: ['name'],
  sortAscending: true,
  itemController: 'product'
});
```

The products controller is present at app/controllers/products.js

As the products controller needs to work on a list of products, it should extend `Ember.ArrayController`. `Ember.ArrayController` includes the `Ember.SortableMixin` that implements the sorting of the items present in the model property of the controller. `Ember.SortableMixin` uses two properties to sort the underlying elements.

The first one is `sortProperties`, which contains an array of properties on which the items should be sorted. In our case, we sort the items in the table according to their names. The second property read by `Ember.SortableMixin` is `sortAscending`, which is a boolean variable which tells whether to use ascending order or descending order while sorting the elements.

Now, since `ArrayController` works on a complete array and not on individual items, the functionality to format date, description, and dimensions can't go in here. The products controller will contain properties that work on the array as a whole; for example, if we had to show how many products are above $50, we would add the computed property in the products controller.

For an individual item-specific transformation, the `Ember.ArrayController` can contain an `itemController` property, which should point to the controller that needs to be used for every item in the list. As you can see in the preceding code sample, we point `itemController` to the `product`. This tells the Ember.js framework to use `product` controller to decorate each of the item present in the `model` array.

Let's look at `app/controllers/products/product.js`, that is, the `product` controller that contains the computed properties decorating the original properties received from the `severof` individual items present in the `model` array:

```
import Ember from "ember";

export default Ember.ObjectController.extend({
```

```
formattedPrice: function(){
  returnthis.get('symbol') + "    " +
    $.number(this.get('price'),2);
}.property('symbol','price'),

formattedDimension: function(){
  returnthis.get('dimensions.width') + " x " +
    this.get('dimensions.height') + " x " +
    this.get('dimensions.length');
}.property('dimensions.width','dimensions.height',
  'dimensions.length'),

shortDescription: function(){
  varshortDesc = this.get('description').substring(0, 25);
  returnshortDesc + "...";

}.property('description')
});
```

Product controller is present at app/controllers/products/product.js

The product controller defined above extends Ember.ObjectController and works on an individual item of the array as its model property. Here, you can see that we have defined three computed properties: formattedPrice, formattedDimension, and shortDescription. These computed properties transform the data and make it presentable to the end user.

Now, since we have defined all the controllers and routes, the only thing left is to display the list of items in the products template. So, let's create the products template and present the products data in a tabular form, as shown in the following:

```
<h1> Products </h1>
<table class="table table-bordered">
  <thead>
    <tr>
      <th data-field="name">Item</th>
      <th data-field="description">Description</th>
      <th data-field="dimension">Dimension</th>
      <th data-field="price">Price</th>
    </tr>
    {{#each product in controller}}
    <tr>
      <td>{{product.name}}</td>
      <td>{{product.shortDescription}}</td>
      <td>{{product.formattedDimension}}</td>
      <td>{{product.formattedPrice}}</td>
```

```
      {{/each}}
    <tr>
  </thead>
</table>
```

The products template is present at app/templates/products.hbs

In the `products.hbs` template, we iterate over every item present in the products controller and present the transformed data from the product controller. `itemController` enables us to use `{{product.shortDescription}}` without much of configuration. This keeps the code clean and easy to understand.

If you go inside the `chapter5/example1` directory and run `ember serve`, you will see the following output at `http://localhost:4200`:

Menu ≡	Products			
example1 🏠	Item	Description	Dimension	Price
	Leather Jacket	A very long jacket descti...	12 x 9.5 x 7	$ 2,000.00
	Some Coat	A very long coat desction...	11 x 10 x 8	€ 300.00
	T Shirt	A very long T Shirt desct...	13 x 11 x 9	$ 59.00
	White Shirt	A very long Shirt desctio...	14 x 12 x 10	£ 2,000.00

Presenting a list of products using Ember.ArrayController

Connecting controllers

Sometimes, especially in nested routes, the nested controller would want access to the model or data from the parent controller. The Ember.js framework provides us with the ability to link two or more controllers together so that the state of one controller can be accessed from the other one. Such a link between two controllers is not limited to only nested routes, but to any controller that wants to access another controller.

Let us see this in an example. We will continue with our preceding example of showing a list of products to end users. After creating a view to show all the products in a tabular form, let's move on to creating a page for an individual product and another one to show the reviews for a specific product.

Let's start by adding the routes in `app/router.js`, as follows:

```
Router.map(function() {
  this.resource("products");
  this.resource("product",{path: "/:id"},function(){
```

```
        this.route("reviews");
    });

});
```

Router code is present at app/router.js

After adding in the two additions in `router.js`, let's move on to creating the corresponding routes as follows:

```
import Ember from "ember";

export default Ember.Route.extend({
  model: function(params){
    return {"id": 1, "name" : "Leather Jacket" , "description" :
      "A very long jacket description which cannot be shown
      inside a table and will have to be shortened",
      "currency": "USD" , "symbol": "$" , "price":"1999.999" ,
      "dimensions": {"length": 7.0,"width": 12.0,"height": 9.5}
    }
  }
});
```

Product route is present at app/routes/product.js

The product route is straightforward and self-explanatory.

Let's look at the `reviews` route in the following:

```
import Ember from "ember";

export default Ember.Route.extend({
  model: function(){
    return ["This is a great jaket","Another
      Review","AwesomeJacket","Too pricy"];
  }
});
```

The product/reviews route is present at app/routes/product/reviews.js

The reviews route is simple and returns the reviews related to a product. Here, we always return a static list of reviews. In a real scenario, you would fetch the reviews related to a product from the server.

Let's look at the `reviews` controller:

```
import Ember from "ember";

export default Ember.ArrayController.extend({
```

```
    needs:["product"],
    product: Ember.computed.alias("controllers.product")
});
```

The product/reviews controller is present at app/controllers/product/reviews.js

The Ember.js framework provides us with the needs keyword to manage dependencies between controllers. The `needs` property expects the names of controllers that the current controller wants access to. In our case, we need to show the name of the product for which the review has to been written. Now, since the product object is set in the model property of the product controller, we would need access to the product controller to fetch the name of the product for which the review has been written.

The controllers made available by the `needs` property can be accessed by using the `controllers.product` convention. To make it simpler, we make an alias product, pointing to `controllers.product`.

Now, to access the name of the product for which the review has been written, we can use `{{product.name}}`:

```
<h2> Reviews for {{product.name}}</h2>
<table class="table table-bordered">
  <thead>
    <tr>
      <th data-field="name">Reviews</th>
    </tr>
    {{#each review in controller}}
    <tr>
      <td>{{review}}</td>
    </tr>
    {{/each}}
  </thead>
</table>
```

The reviews template is present at app/templates/product/reviews.js

Unlike traditional MVC frameworks, the controllers in the Ember.js framework are singleton, which means that during a browser session, the same instance of controller is returned and shared across the application. Whenever you change your route, the controller is not destroyed and keeps its state intact. When the user interacts with the application only, the model is fetched again and the template bound to the route is updated with the correct data.

Summary

In this chapter, you learned about the Ember.js controllers. You saw that the Ember.js controllers serve their purpose fully when used to make models available to templates and maintain a nonpersistent state. You learned about how templates, controllers, and models interact with each other and how the framework segregates these components to effectively design your application around that. Then, you saw how `Ember.ObjectController` and `Ember.ArrayController` help in decorating a single object and an array of objects, respectively. In the end, you learned about how to manage dependencies between different controllers by using the needs property. In the next chapter, you will see how to make your Ember.js application effectively talk with the backend API server.

6
Communicating with the API Server Using ember-data

In the last chapter, we learned about the Ember.js controllers. We learned about how to decorate our models with view-specific business logic using Ember.js controllers. In this chapter, we shall improve our understanding of how to effectively communicate with the backend server using `ember-data` library.

In this chapter, we shall cover:

- Introducing ember-data
- Defining ember-data models:
  - Defining relationships between your ember-data models
  - One-to-one
  - One-to-many
  - Many-to-many
- Understanding the ember-data identity map – DS.Store
- Working with records:
  - Finding the records
  - Modifying the records
- The default REST adapter and serializer:
  - Sideloaded relationships
  - Customizing the DS.RESTAdapter
  - Customizing the URL endpoints
- Example application

Introducing ember-data

Models form the core of any MVC design pattern as they describe the core business domain at hand. In Ember.js, every route has an associated model that describes the business domain that the route needs to work on. Almost all of the examples that we have seen so far operate on the static data that is returned from the model property of the routes. But most of the times the data that needs to be operated upon is not static and is fetched from a remote server.

Traditionally we have used jQuery or plain JavaScript to fetch the data from the server, using AJAX calls and then using those returned JSON objects as models in our application. This approach works well for applications that are simpler in nature, but very quickly get difficult to maintain when working on domains that are complex in nature, especially the ones that have relationships among them. We need to make sure that the correct relationship is linked and updated in our application.

The `ember-data` library tries to solve the problems highlighted earlier that are encountered in building single page web applications, by providing a standard way of accessing, finding, modifying, and saving the model objects of your application. By using the `ember-data` library, you can easily simplify your code that handles the communication with the backend server, by letting ember-data handle most of the complexity for you. This lets you focus more on solving the business problem at hand. The library also brings in a lot of optimizations to your code that improve the overall performance of your application.

Ember Data is designed to be agnostic to the underlying storage technique, and hence it works equally well will HTTP based JSON API, as well as streaming WebSockets.

The `ember-data` library is actively being developed and improved, and is under the beta quality. The API is highly stabilized and there are a lot of companies who have been using ember-data in production for quite some time now.

The current beta of `ember-data` is already included with Ember CLI and can be checked from the `bower.json` file, present in the project's root directory.

Defining ember-data models

As discussed in the introduction, models in any MVC application define the business domain properties and behavior that needs to be consumed by the end user of your application. As we learned from the *Injecting the model for your template* section, in Chapter 4, *Managing Application State Using Ember.js Routes* that models, these could either be plain static JavaScript objects, or JSON data that is fetched from a remote server.

Model objects, defined by the `ember-data` library abstracts away the complexities involved with handling the communication with the server, serializing, as well as de-serializing of the response received from the server. In order to define your `ember-data` model object, you just need to extend the `DS.Model` object present in `ember-data` module as follows:

```
import DS from "ember-data";

export default DS.Model.extend({
  title: DS.attr('string'),
  isbn: DS.attr('string'),
  pages: DS.attr('number'),
  description: DS.attr('string'),
  authors: DS.hasMany('author',{ async: true }),
  publisher: DS.belongsTo('publisher',{ async: true }),
  reviews: DS.hasMany("review",{ async: true })
});
```

The book model is present at chapter6/example1/app/models/book.js

As you can see in the preceding code, we created a new file in `app/models` directory with the name `book.js`. The book object has a few differences from the objects we have seen so far.

The book object extends the `DS.Model` object, instead of `Ember.Object`. The `DS.Model` class inherits itself from the `Ember.Object` class; as a result, you can use all the features provided by `Ember.Object`, including computed properties and observers. The `DS.Model` class also adds in other additional capabilities, including serializing, deserializing a record, and saving it back to the server.

Model attributes in `DS.Model` objects are also handled differently, as the library needs to know which properties need to be serialized when sending them to the server, and which properties to de-serialize when receiving the response from the server. As a result, a `DS.Model` object can have both types of properties: the ones that need to be synced with the server, and also the ones that are very specific to how you want to present the data to the end user, and not sync it back to the server. Model attributes that have to be serialized and deserialized from the server are assigned a type `DS.attr()`. The `DS.attr` takes in an optional argument defining the type of attribute. The currently supported attribute types are string, number, boolean, and date. When nothing is passed as an argument to `DS.attr`, then the library tries to automatically identify the type received from the server, and deserializes it. You can also pass in any default value that you need to set on the attribute by passing an optional second argument to the `DS.attr` method, such as the following:

```
DS.attr('boolean', {defaultValue: false})
```

Defining relationships between your ember-data models

When defining model objects in your application, you may realize the need to refer or link two models together, something very similar to what you do in relational databases. Ember Data lets you do that in a very easy manner by providing support for the several possible relationship types that two models can have with each other.

Currently, three types of relationships are supported in `ember-data`:

- One-to-one
- One-to-many
- Many-to-many

Let's see what each relationship types mean, and how to define it in your model objects.

One-to-one

The one to one type of relationship means that the model attribute is linked to one, and only one, object. In Ember Data, you can link an attribute to one other object by using the `DS.belongsTo` method. The `DS.belongsTo` takes in two arguments, the first one in a mandatory argument, specifying the name of the object the attribute links to, and the second argument is an object containing properties to inform the adapter on how to load the object when a response is received from the server. One such property is `async`. If you set the `async` property to `true`, `{ async: true }`, it signals the `DS.RESTAdapter` (and other types of adapters if they respect this option) that the relationships of this model have to be fetched asynchronously. We will discuss more about loading relationships when we discuss the `DS.RESTAdapter`.

One example of one to one mapping would be mapping an address type to user type, such as in the following example:

```
app/models/user.js

import DS from "ember-data";

export default DS.Model.extend({
  name: DS.attr("string"),
```

```
    address: DS.belongsTo('address')
});
```

```
app/models/address.js
```

```
import DS from "ember-data";
```

```
export default DS.Model.extend({
  street: DS.attr("string"),
  locality: DS.attr("string"),
  houseNo: DS.attr("number"),
  user: DS.belongsTo('user')
});
```

The example signifies that there is a direct mapping between a user and an address. A user can have only one address, and an address can have only one user.

One-to-many

The one to many relationship type, as the names suggests, means that a model attribute is of type array, and can have many models of one type linked to that property.

Continuing with our book example, a book can have many reviews linked to it but on the other hand, a review will only belong to one, and only one, book. This can be modeled in ember-data using DS.hasMany() as an attribute type. DS.hasMany like DS.belongsTo can take in two arguments, the first one being a mandatory one, depicting the name of the relationship, and the second one being an optional argument that tells the adapter how to load the relationships of the object.

Let's understand this with the following example:

```
// File: app/models/book.js
import DS from "ember-data";

export default DS.Model.extend({
  title: DS.attr('string'),
  isbn: DS.attr('string'),
  pages: DS.attr('number'),
  description: DS.attr('string'),
  authors: DS.hasMany('author'),
  publisher: DS.belongsTo('publisher'),
  reviews: DS.hasMany("review")
});
```

The book model is present at chapter6/example1/app/models/book.js

You can see in the code that a book's attribute `reviews` are assigned a type of `DS.hasMany("reviews")`, which means that the book is linked to reviews via has-many relationship type.

Similarly, in order to refer a book back from a review, we will need a `DS.belongsTo('book')` relationship type defined inside the `review` class, as follows:

```
import DS from "ember-data";

export default DS.Model.extend({
  name: DS.attr("string"),
  comment: DS.attr("string"),
  book: DS.belongsTo("book")
});
```

The review model is present at chapter6/example1/app/models/review.js

Many-to-many

A many-to-many relationship type is the one in which one object can have an attribute that links to zero or more instances of another object, and vice versa. For example, a book can have many authors linked to it, and an author can write one or more books. Let's make this clearer by using an example:

```
// File: app/models/book.js
import DS from "ember-data";

export default DS.Model.extend({
  title: DS.attr('string'),
  isbn: DS.attr('string'),
  pages: DS.attr('number'),
  description: DS.attr('string'),
authors: DS.hasMany('author'),
  publisher: DS.belongsTo('publisher'),
reviews: DS.hasMany("review")
});
```

The book model is present at chapter6/example1/app/models/book.js

As you can see here, a book is linked with authors by using `DS.hasMany('author')`, which means that the author is an array that could refer to zero or more authors.

Similarly, an author can have a similar relationship with the book type, as follows:

```
import DS from "ember-data";

export default DS.Model.extend({
  firstName: DS.attr('string'),
  lastName: DS.attr('string'),
  fullName: function() {
return this.get('firstName') + ' ' + this.get('lastName');
  }.property('firstName', 'lastName'),
  bio: DS.attr('string'),
  books: DS.hasMany('book')
});
```

The author model is present at chapter6/example1/app/models/author.js

Here, you can see that the author refers back to the book type using `book: DS.hasMany('book')`.

As you saw, Ember Data makes it very easy to define relationships between your models. Defining relationships amongst different model objects keeps your code clean and easy to understand. Making proper relationships among your model objects also helps you enforce the **Single Responsibility Principle**, which states that "Every class should have a single responsibility, and that responsibility should be entirely encapsulated by the class. All its services should be narrowly aligned with that responsibility."

Understanding the ember-data identity map – DS.Store

Before we move on to creation and persistence of the model objects defined in the previous section, we need to understand a very core part of `ember-data` library, the `Store`.

`DS.Store` or simply **store**, is a central repository that contains all the data of the model objects that were fetched from the server. It is also responsible for managing the life cycle of the instances of `DS.Model` types. This includes creating instances of `DS.Model` class, searching, saving, updating, and deleting records to the server.

 The instances of `DS.Model` types are also known as records, and whenever we use the word records they will imply the same.

The instance of DS.Store is automatically created, and is made available as a property to all the components of your application. This happens when the ember-data library is loaded. Normally, an Ember.js application will have only one instance of DS.Store, which is shared across the application.

The store also acts like an in-memory cache for your application. If a record that was just fetched from the server is asked to be fetched again, then the store will return the same object that is already present in the cache that was fetched recently, rather than making another an HTTP call to the server to fetch the record again. This minimizes the network calls made to the server, and hence renders the template that displays the record quickly. This behavior, in which the store always returns the same object when the search parameters provided to it are same, is known as an **identity map**, and hence DS.Store is also referred as an identity map.

Let's see what happens when you send a request to fetch a record to be displayed in your template:

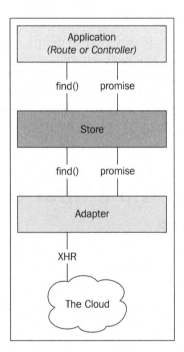

This depicts the flow when your application asks the store to fetch a record from the server

When your application requests the store to find a record for a given ID or a condition, the store will first check whether or not the record is already present in its cache. If it's not present, then the store will ask the adapter to fetch the record for it.

Adapter in `ember-data` is an object that actually communicates with the backend server. It knows about how and what calls it needs to make to the server to fetch the data. For example, if the store asks the REST adapter to fetch a book with the ID 2 for it, a REST adapter shall follow the REST conventions while making the call to the server. It shall translate that request into an `HTTP GET` call with URL `/books/2` to the server. When an adapter in an asynchronous world is not able to return the result to the store immediately, so they instead of returning the actual object the adapter immediately returns a promise to the store which is resolved once the adapter receives the actual JSON data from the server. Similar to this is when the application asks the store for a record that is not present in the store. The store returns a promise to the application, which is resolved when the adapter sends the data received from the server to the store. On receiving the JSON data from the adapter, the store initializes the model object from the data returned, and the template that is bound to the record is updated with the latest data fetched from the server.

On the other hand, if the store receives a request for a record that is present in its cache, the store resolves the promise immediately, and presents the retrieved object to the application.

Working with records

As we now have some understanding of how a store works, let's see how we can use the store to create and delete a record.

To create a new record, you can use the `createRecord` method present on the instance of `DS.Store`. In your controller or route, you can get the reference of the store object by calling `this.store`. Let's take a look at the following example, to know how to create a record of type book:

```
var book = this.store.createRecord('book', {
  title: "Ember.js Essentials",
  isbn: "ISBN1",
  pages: 180,
  description: "The Essentials required to master Ember.js"
});
```

As you may have figured out, the `createRecordfunction` takes in two arguments; the first one is the name of the model object you want to instantiate, which is `book` in our case, and the second one being the object with properties set to their values. Normally, the users of your application will be entering these attributes in a form, whose values will be bound to the model attributes.

As you may have noticed, we did not set the relationships of the books here. The ember-data library currently has one limitation; if you assign any promises to relationships of your object, it doesn't automatically resolve them, and assign the resolved object(s) as the value of the property. So, we need to make sure that the relationships should not be assigned to a promise and hence, the object to which it is assigned should contain actual values.

So, we could do something like the following:

```
var author = this.store.createRecord("author",{
  firstName: "Suchit",
  lastName: "Puri",
  bio: "something interesting about me",
  book: book
});
```

Now, since one book can have more than one author, we modeled it using the has-many relationship. As a result, the author's property becomes an empty array on which we need to insert our author object, as follows:

```
book.get("authors").addObject(author);
```

Similarly, you can create a record for the publisher, and then assign it with a book, which is a many to one relationship, because a publisher can publish many books, but a book will be published by only one publisher. Let's take a look at the following example:

```
var packt = this.store.createRecord('publisher',{
  name: "Packt Publushing",
  organizationName: "Pact",
  address: "London"
});

packt.get("books").pushObject(book);
book.set('publisher',packt);
```

As you may have noticed by now, a DS.hasMany relationship results an array being initialized for that attribute. One important thing to note is that the ember-data library makes the DS.hasMany attribute as a read-only property. This means that you cannot assign the attribute to a new array. Let's see what happens when you try to set the hasMany association property, books, to an array while creating a new publisher record.

```
var packt = this.createRecord('publisher',{
  name: "Packt Publishing",
```

```
    organizationName: "Packt",
    address: "London",
    books:[book]
});
```

Doing the above will result in an error `cannot set read-only property`.

Let's see how you can delete a record from the store. The `DS.Store` maintains a flag `isDeletedfor` for every object stored in its cache. When you make a request to delete the record from the cache, the store just sets the flag and then does not return the record in future queries. To delete a record, you just need to call the `deleteRecord` method on the object.

Doing `book.deleteRecord();` will remove the object from the store and set the `isDeletedflag` for the object. To sync the changes to the server, you will have to call the save method on the object, which, if used with the default `DS.RESTAdapter`, shall make a `DELETE` call `/books/{:id}` to the server.

 One very important thing to note here is that in both cases of creating a new record and deleting a record, you will have to make a save call on the object to reflect the changes on the server. The `save()` method will make an appropriate `POST` or `DELETE` call, based on the state of the object to the server, to sync the state of the object with the server.

If you are using the `DS.RESTAdapter`, once you create a new record and save it to the server, making any further changes to the object will result in a `PUT` call to the server. So, if you make any changes to the book object after saving it the `ember-data` library, you would make a `PUT` call to `/books/:id` to update the record and sync it with the server.

Whenever we make a save call to the server to sync the state of the object with that of the server, the save immediately returns a promise object, which is resolved once you get a response from the server. Hence, it is a good practice to use them while saving a record on the server as follows:

```
book.save().then(function(book){
  //Do something useful here

}).catch(function(reason){
  //handle the error if any
});
```

Finding the records

Till now, we have seen how to create, delete, and update a record in `ember-data`, and how to sync the record with the server. Often, you may just want to fetch the records from the server based on some criteria, and then display the list or record and then display the list of records fetched. The `ember-data` library provides us with the `find` method to help us locate our records.

The `find` method takes in two arguments; the first argument is the name of the entity or the model we are looking for. This is a required argument. The second argument is either an ID or an object that describes the query we need to use while finding the record. One very important characteristic of the `find` method is that if the record(s) that we are looking for is not found in the store's cache, the `find` method will immediately return a promise object instead of the actual object. The actual object is initialized with the values from the server, once the promise is resolved. Let's look at an example to make it clearer.

To look for all the books on the server we shall make a call `this.store.find("book")`. This shall get translated into a GET request to `/books`, which returns a list of all the books present on the server.

To just look for all the books in the cache of the store, we make a call:

```
this.store.all("book")
```

This command will not make any network calls and only looks for records of type `book` in the cache of the store.

Similarly, to search for any record on the server of a specific ID, we make a call:

```
this.store.find("book",1)
```

This will result in a network call GET to `/books/1`, which should return the complete book object with ID 1.

To look for a book object by name, we need to pass in the query object as the second parameter to the find method, as follows:

```
this.store.find("book",{"name":"Ember.js Essentials"})
```

This will result in a GET request `/book?name='Ember.js Essentials'` made to the server.

Please note that all the URLs mentioned are according to the default convention of `DS.RESTAdapter`.

As we learned in *Chapter 4, Managing Application State Using Ember.js Routes* that a route can override the model hook and return the model object that the templates will bind to. One important thing to note here is that if you return a promise from the model hook of the router, the router will not transition to the route, and render the template till the promise is resolved.

Modifying the records

Once you have retrieved or saved a record from the server, you can change its properties in your Ember application. The `ember-data` library maintains a flag, called as `isDirty`, to check if the record was modified after it was retrieved from the server, as follows:

```
var book = this.store.createRecord('book',{
  title: "Ember.js Essentials",
  isbn: "ISBN1",
  pages: 180,
  description: "The Essentials required to master Ember.js"
});

book.save().then(function(book){
  console.log(book.get('isDirty')); //False
  book.set('isbn','new ISBN');
  console.log(book.get('isDirty')); //True
  console.log(book.changedAttributes()); //{isbn:['ISBN1','new
    ISBN']}
});
```

Once we save a book, then subsequently editing it, like changing any property of the book, will result in setting the `isDirty` flag to true.

Another helpful method available on the `DS.Model` object is `changedAttributes()`. This method will return an object containing the attributes of the model that were changed since the last sync with the server.

The default REST adapter and serializer

As we saw in the section, *Understanding the Ember Data identity map – DS.Store*, all interactions with the server are handled by the **adapter**. Adapter in `ember-data` understands how to connect to the server, in order to fetch and save the records from/to the server. Similarly, `serializer`, as the name implies, is responsible for serializing or converting the response received from the server to `DS.Model` objects.

By default in `ember-data`, the store will use the `DS.RESTAdapter` and `DS.RESTSerializer`. As the name implies, the `DS.RESTAdapter` is based on the **REST (Representational State Transfer)** principles to load or save a record from/to the server. The `DS.RESTAdapter` communicates with the HTTP server by sending and receiving **JSON (JavaScript Object Notation)** data, via AJAX requests. If the server with which the Ember.js application talks with, understands and follows the URL conventions according to REST principles, then your `ember-data` communication will work flawlessly without any customization to the adapter or serializer.

Let us see what the URL endpoints for our book model (`chapter-6/example1/app/models/book.js`) discussed when used with different actions:

Action	HTTP Verb	URL
Find	GET	/books/2
Find All	GET	/books
Update	PUT	/books/2
Create	POST	/books
Delete	DELETE	/books/2

The URL endpoints which DS.RESTAdapter makes call to when used with different actions

As you can see, the `DS.RESTAdapter` uses plural form of the model name to create the URLs, hence the URL for the `book` model becomes /books/. Another important thing to note here is the use of HTTP verbs while making calls to the server. To fetch a record or records from the server, the adapter uses GET verb or action; to create a new record, the POST verb is used; to update an existing record, the PUT verb is used; and to delete a record, the DELETE verb is used.

Now that we have understood how the adapter creates the URLs to communicate with the server, let's understand how we need to send the JSON response back from the server, in order for it to be compliant with the `DS.RESTAdapter` and `DS.RESTSerializer`.

In order to understand the JSON response from the server, let us take the look at the book model:

```
import DS from "ember-data";

export default DS.Model.extend({
  title: DS.attr('string'),
  isbn: DS.attr('string'),
  pages: DS.attr('number'),
  description: DS.attr('string'),
  authors: DS.hasMany('author',{ async: true }),
```

```
    publisher: DS.belongsTo('publisher',{ async: true }),
    reviews: DS.hasMany("review",{ async: true })
});
```

The book model is present at chapter6/example1/app/models/book.js

Here, you can see that the book model contains both attributes and relationships. When we make a call to fetch a particular book from the server using `store.find("book",1)`, this gets translated to `GET /books/1` that should return a JSON response, which can be de-serialized into `book` model object. The JSON response returned from the server should be of the following structure:

```
{
  "book": {
    "id":1
    "title": "Ember.js Essentials",
    "isbn": "ISBN1",
    "pages": 180,
    "description": "Ember.js essentials to master",
    "authors": [1],
    "publisher": 1,
    "reviews": [1,2,3]
  }
}
```

Here, you can see that we return a JSON response that has a top-level key that is the same as the name of the model, `book` in our case. This is followed by the attributes and their values. One important thing to note is that it is mandatory to send the ID of the object with the JSON response, the `ID` attribute is defined automatically on every `DS.Model` object and is used by the store to uniquely identify the records.

Let's look at relationships now. The book record has three relationships, namely authors, publisher, and reviews. The relationships of `DS.hasMany` type use the plural form of the model and expect the relationship IDs in an array.

The relationship response `"reviews": [1,2,3]` tells the serializer that this book object has three reviews, whose IDs are 1, 2, and 3. Similarly, the `"publisher": 1` tells the adapter and serializer that a book has one publisher with ID 1.

Now, as we used `{async:true}` in defining our relationships of the `book` model, the `DS.RESTAdapter` and `DS.RESTSerializer` that the JSON response of the book object will only contain the IDs of the relationships in proper format. These relationship objects (authors, publisher and reviews) should be fetched separately only when they are referred to by the application code. When such references to the relationships are encountered, a call `store.find('reviews',1)` or `GET /reviews/1` is sent for each object present in the `"reviews": [1,2,3]` array.

The `async` property is very helpful in cases where an object has a lot of relationships, but initially only the details of the objects are visible on the screen as the relationships are fetched lazily when required by the application.

Sideloaded relationships

Till now, we have seen the response structure when relationships are defined with `{async: true}`. There could be cases when you don't want this behavior, and want to load the complete object in one go. This is also the default behavior of the relationships in `ember-data` library. Let us see how we should structure the response in order for it to load the book object with its associated relationships synchronously, in one go.

For side loading the relationships, we will have to define the `book` model without the `async` property set to true in its relationships, as follows:

```
import DS from "ember-data";
export default DS.Model.extend({
  title: DS.attr('string'),
  isbn: DS.attr('string'),
  pages: DS.attr('number'),
  description: DS.attr('string'),
  authors: DS.hasMany('author'),
  publisher: DS.belongsTo('publisher'),
  reviews: DS.hasMany("review")
});
```

The side-loaded response from the server should be of the following structure:

```
{
  "book": {
    "id":1,
    "title": "Ember.js Essentials",
    "isbn": "ISBN1",
    "pages": 180,
    "description": "Ember.js essentials to master",
    "authors": [1],
    "publisher": 1,
    "reviews": [1,2,3]
  },

  "publisher": {
    "id": 1,
    "name": "Packt Publishing",
    "organizationName": "Pact",
```

```
      "address":"Packt Publishing London",
      "book":1
    },

    "authors": [{
      "id": 1,
      "firstName": "firstName1",
      "lastName" : "LastName1",
      "bio": "Great Guy",
      "book":[1]
    }],
    "reviews": [{
      "id": 1
      "name": "Reviewer 1",
      "comment": "comment 1",
      "book":1
    },{
      "id": 2
      "name": "Reviewer 2",
      "comment": "comment 2",
      "book":1
    },
    {
      "id": 3
      "name": "Reviewer 3",
      "comment": "comment 3",
      "book":1
    }]
  }
```

In the preceding response, you can see that instead of sending just the `book` `object`JSON, we also side load the relationships of the `book` model that is, we also side load the `publisher`, `authors`, and `reviews`. Please note that all `DS.hasMany` relationships are provided as array of objects, and `DS.belongsTo` relationships are provided as single objects.

Customizing the DS.RESTAdapter

Till now, we have discussed the behavior of the default DS.RESTAdapter, but there are situations, especially when integration with API which is not fully compliant with REST conventions, which require to customize and modify the adapter, according to your needs. When using Ember CLI, all the customizations of the adapter go in app/adapters/ directory. You can customize the behavior for the adapter for the whole application as well as restrict it to only one or more model classes.

Application-wide changes to the adapter should go in app/adapters/application. js, and any model specific customizations should go in app/adapters/<name of the model>.js, just as if we had to customize the adapter for only the book model, we would have created an adapter for it in app/adapters/book.js.

Customizing the URL endpoints

If you want to define any prefix that is prepended to the URL, you can do that by defining the namespace property of your adapter.

```
import DS from 'ember-data';
export default DS.RESTAdapter.extend({
  namespace: 'api'
});
```

Application adapter using custom namespace is present at chapter-6/example1/app/adapters/application.js

Setting the namespace property of the application adapter will prefix all the generated URL for all the models of the application with api, for example this. store.find ("book",1) will now become /api/books/1, instead of /books/1. If your API server runs on a different domain or you are integrating with third party APIs directly from your Ember.js application, you will need to change the host name while building the URLs for your data models.

You can do that by setting the host property of the adapter as follows:

```
import DS from 'ember-data';
export default DS.RESTAdapter.extend({
  host: 'http://api.someotherdomain.com/'
});
```

By setting the host property of the adapter, the call for this.store.find ("book",1) will now go to http://api.someotherdomain.com/books/1 instead of just /books/1, which goes to the same server that hosts your Ember.js application.

Please note here that in order for the above functionality of cross-domain functionality to work properly, you will have use a browser that supports **CORS** (**cross-origin resource sharing**), and you will have to configure the server to send in the correct CORS headers.

By default, Ember Data comes with a few more adapters other than `DS.RESTAdapter`, which are mentioned as follows:

- `DS.FixtureAdapter` – This adapter is used primarily for testing the model classes. The fixture adapters don't make the actual calls to the backend server but serve the model data from the fixtures already loaded and configured in the memory.

- `DS.Adapter` – This is base adapter class, it does not implement any functionality but is primarily used as a contract to implement new adapters.

- `DS.ActiveModelAdapter` – This adapter extends the default `DS.RESTAdapter` and hence most of the features and conventions remain the same, here. The main benefit of this adapter is that it works well with the Ruby on Rails active model serializer.

Example application

Now that we have discussed different aspects of the ember-data library, let's look at a real example for the same.

The source code for the example can be found at `https://github.com/suchitpuri/emberjs-essentials/tree/master/chapter-6/example1`. In this example, we are aiming to continue with the books model that was defined in the chapter, and work on the following functionality:

1. Create a new book and its related author and publisher.
2. View a book's information, including its related publisher, authors, and reviews.
3. View the list of all books in our catalog.

Here, to communicate with the backend server, we have used the HTTP-mock generators provided by Ember CLI to generate mock responses. The HTTP-mock generator generates the Express.js (found at `http://expressjs.com/`)server scaffold for the resource. If you want to generate a REST compliant URL for your resource, you can do that by running the following command at your project's root directory. This is `chapter-6/example1` in our case:

```
ember g http-mock <resource name>
```

For the current example, we have already generated the HTTP mock calls for our resources. You can see the mock calls at `chapter-6/example1/server/mocks` directory.

This is how the mock calls for the book resource look:

```
module.exports = function(app) {
  var express = require('express');
  var booksRouter = express.Router();

  booksRouter.get('/', function(req, res) {
    res.send({
      "books": [{
        "id":1,
        "title": "Ember.js Essentials",
        "isbn": "ISBN1",
        "pages": 180,
        "description": "Ember.js essentials to master",
        "authors": [1],
        "publisher": 1,
        "reviews": [1,2,3]
      },
      {
        "id":2,
        "title": "Some Other Book On Ember.js",
        "isbn": "ISBN2",
        "pages": 200,
        "description": "Some Description",
        "authors": [2],
        "publisher": 1,
        "reviews": [4,5,6]
      }]
    });
  });
  booksRouter.post('/', function(req, res) {
    res.status(201);
    res.send({"book":{
      "id":Math.floor(Math.random()*1000)
    }});
  });
  booksRouter.get('/:id', function(req, res) {
    var reviews,authors, publisher;
    if(req.params.id == 1){
      reviews = [1,2,3]
      authors = [1]
```

```
      publisher = 1
    }else if(req.params.id == 2){
      reviews = [4,5,6]
      authors = [2]
      publisher = 2
    }
    res.send({
      "book": {
        "id":req.params.id,
        "title": "Ember.js Essentials",
        "isbn": "ISBN1",
        "pages": 180,
        "description": "Ember.js essentials to master",
        "authors": authors,
        "publisher": publisher,
        "reviews": reviews
      }
    });
  });
  booksRouter.put('/:id', function(req, res) {
    res.send({
      "book": {
        "id": req.params.id
      }
    });
  });
  booksRouter.delete('/:id', function(req, res) {
    res.status(204).end();
  });
  app.use('/api/books', booksRouter);
};
```

The mock calls for the book resource is present at chapter-6/example1/server/mocks/books.js

A full explanation of the above Express.js code is beyond the scope of the book, but as this is just JavaScript code, it is not that difficult to understand. The only thing to note here is that we have mapped different HTTP verbs, with different JSON responses here.

Similar to the above code, we have created mocked responses for authors, publishers, and reviews too.

Let us now see the Ember application code that is present at `chapter-6/example1/` `app/` directory.

The adapter's directory contains the application adapter in `application.js` as follows:

```
import DS from 'ember-data';
export default DS.RESTAdapter.extend({
  namespace: 'api'
});
```

The application adapter is present at chapter-6/example1/app/adapters/application.js

Here, we just define the namespace of our server API.

All the model classes are present at `chapter-6/example1/app/models/`:

```
import DS from "ember-data";

export default DS.Model.extend({
  title: DS.attr('string'),
  isbn: DS.attr('string'),
  pages: DS.attr('number'),
  description: DS.attr('string'),
  authors: DS.hasMany('author',{ async: true }),
  publisher: DS.belongsTo('publisher',{ async: true }),
  reviews: DS.hasMany("review",{ async: true })
});
```

The book model is present at chapter-6/example1/app/models/book.js

Let us see the routes that we have defined in our application:

```
Router.map(function() {
  this.resource('books', function(){
    this.route('book',{path: "/:id"});
    this.route('new');
  });
});
```

The router.js is present at chapter-6/example1/app/router.js

As you can see, we have defined a books resource, which has two additional routes: `books.book` and `books.new`.

The `books.book` route should show the information for a specific book and hence we should ask the store about the book with the matching ID to be returned from its model hook:

```
import Ember from 'ember';

export default Ember.Route.extend({
  model: function(params){
    return this.store.find('book',params.id);
  }
});
```

The books.book route is present at chapter-6/example1/app/routes/books/book.js

Similarly, in our books index route, we would want to return all the books in our collection. So, we should return an array of books from its model hook:

```
import Ember from 'ember';

export default Ember.Route.extend({
    model: function(){
        return this.store.find('book');
    }
});
```

The books.index route is present at chapter-6/example1/app/routes/books/index.js

To create a new book, we need to define the `books.new` template and route. The template for creating a new book is a collection for different input fields to collect data for book, publisher, and author. It also has button that calls the action, `createBook`.

The template for `books.new`, along with `books.book` and `books.index`, can be found in the `chapter-6/example1/app/templates/books/` directory.

The `createBook` action defined in `book.new` template can either be defined in the respective controller or route. But, as we are dealing with saving a resource on the server, the `books.new` route is more natural place to house the action, as follows:

```
import Ember from 'ember';

export default Ember.Route.extend({

  actions:{
    createBook: function(){
```

```
  var that = this;

  var publisher = that.store.createRecord("publisher",{
    "name": that.get("controller.name"),
    "organizationName":
      that.get("controller.organizationName"),
    "address": that.get("controller.address")
  });
  var author = that.store.createRecord("author",{
    "firstName": that.get("controller.firstName"),
    "lastName": that.get("controller.lastName"),
    "bio": that.get("controller.bio")
  });
  var book =  that.store.createRecord("book",{
    "title": that.get("controller.title"),
    "isbn": that.get("controller.isbn"),
    "pages": that.get("controller.pages"),
    "description": that.get("description")
  });
  publisher.save().then(function(publisherFromDB){
    book.set("publisher",publisherFromDB);
    author.save().then(function(authorFromServer){
      //Set The Author to the books
      book.get("authors").then(function(authors){
        authors.pushObject(authorFromServer);
      });
      //Save the book
      book.save().then(function(book){
        that.transitionTo('books.book',book);
      });
    });
  });
}
}
});
```

The books.new route is defined in chapter-6/example1/app/routes/books/new.js

As you can see, we have defined one action, `createBook`, in the actions object of the route. This action is triggered when someone fills from the UI, the book, authors, and publishers information, and presses the `Submit` button.

Inside the createBook action, we first create the objects for publisher, author, and the book. Then we save the publisher by calling save on the record. This would make a POST call to /api/publishers, which would return a response that has a unique ID for the object. When the promise for the publisher.save() resolves successfully, we associate the publisher with the book we are creating.

We do a something similar with the author, and finally, when everything returns successfully for the author resource, we save the book and transition to the book. book route upon successful completion of the save request.

Here's how the books information page will look when you visit/books route:

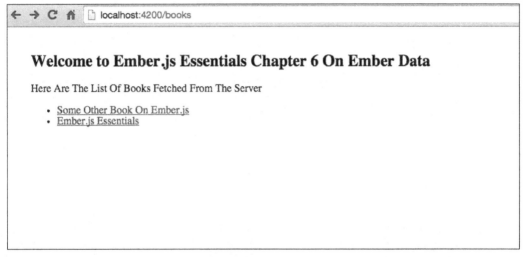

The list of books fetched from the server

When you navigate to the `/books/1`, the book details page will look like this:

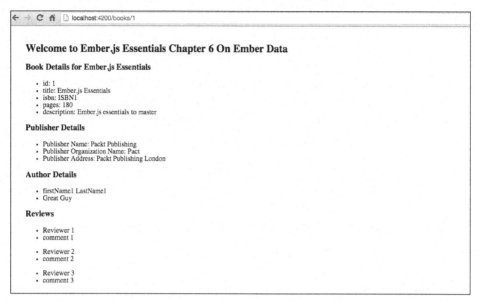

The books details page with all the information

And here's how the book creation form looks when you navigate to /books/new route:

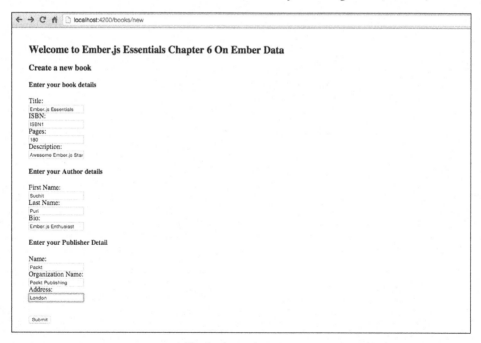

The book creation page

Summary

In this chapter, we learned about the `ember-data` library. We learned how easily and effectively the `ember-data` library design patterns streamline, and how the application communicates with the backend API. We started by defining our own model objects that extend the Ember Data's `DS.Model` class. Then, we considered how to define relationships between our model classes. After defining these relationships, we looked at the identity map provided by the `ember-data` library, the `DS.Store` class. We also learned about the optimization brought in by the data store. After looking at the store, we learned how to create, find, and modify the objects, or records of our model classes. Then, we looked at the default adapter and serializer provided by the `ember-data` library. We also learned how to customize the adapters according to the API we are integrating with. In the end, we looked at an example application that uses `ember-data` to create and fetch records from the API server. In the next chapter, we will talk about building reusable view components in Ember.js.

7
Building Reusable Components

In the last chapter, we learned about the ember-data library. We learned how easily and effectively the ember-data library design patterns streamline, and how the application talks with the backend API. In this chapter, we will focus on building reusable view components using Ember.js views and component classes.

In this chapter, we shall cover:

- Introducing Ember views and components:
  - ° Custom tags with Ember.Component
  - ° Defining your own components
  - ° Passing data to your component

- Providing custom HTML to your components
- Extending Ember.Component:
  - ° Changing your component's tag
  - ° Adding custom CSS classes to your component
  - ° Adding custom attributes to your component's DOM element

- Handling actions for your component
- Mapping component actions to the rest of your application

Introducing Ember views and components

In *Chapter 3, Rendering Using Templates* we learned about handlebars templates and how we can use the Handlebars.js to create data-bound templates. Most of the time, Handlebars.js templates will be enough to create simple applications. But when working on a big, complex application, we are much likely to run into situations in which we can see that we are duplicating a lot of code in handlebars.js templates and repeated handling similar UI events in different controllers of our applications.

In order to tackle the problem of code duplicity and complex event handling of UI elements at one place, Ember.js provides us with two options; components and views. Components and views in Ember.js encapsulate templates, and lets us reuse the abstraction at different places in our application.

Views in Ember.js encapsulate the template and its actions. They have implicit access to the context that the views are being used in. As a result, you can easily access the associated controller and model properties from the view class.

Components, on the other hand, were introduced in Ember in 1.0 RC6 (`http://emberjs.com/blog/2013/06/23/ember-1-0-rc6.html`). Components, as opposed to views, are totally unaware of the context they are being used in. They don't have access to the enclosing controller, route, or model and require all the data to be passed explicitly to them. This makes the reusability of Ember.js components much better than views. Ember.js components are designed to be reusable, not just within your application, but even across different applications.

Since components were introduced in Ember.js framework, there has been a lot of confusion regarding when to use components and when to use views. Initially, the Ember.js framework contained only the `Ember.View` class and all the encapsulation and event handling was done inside it, but when `Ember.Component` was introduced, it was introduced to fix the broken abstraction present in Ember.js views.

Since then, the framework and the community have been pushing to use `Ember.Component` instead of extending `Ember.View`. Even the Ember 2.0 roadmap focuses more on components than it does on views.

As a result, views should be treated as more of an internal implementation detail of Ember.js framework. Views in Ember.js power `{{if}}`, `{{outlet}}`, and many other Handlebars.js helper methods. You should work more with views if you are creating a new Ember.js element, Handlebar.js helper, or are working on a framework of yours that runs alongside Ember.js.

Because of this shift of the framework toward `Ember.Component`, the focus of this chapter will be on Ember components and it will be left to readers to explore ember views for themselves.

Custom tags with Ember.Component

Till now, we have been using built-in HTML tags such as `body`, `tr`, `td`, `div`, and so on in our application. Wouldn't it be nice if a framework could allow you to build application-specific tags whose behavior and actions could be handled using JavaScript? Ember.js `Ember.Component` lets you do that. In fact, the W3C group, which defines the web standards, is already working on a very similar **web component** specification that would allow you to define custom application-specific HTML tags. Once browsers support custom components, you should be able to easily migrate your `Ember.Component` class to the W3C standards.

Defining your own components

The simplest way to define you Ember component is to create a new template file in the `app/templates/components/` folder. In order to resolve the components automatically, the Ember.js framework makes it mandatory for the name of the component's file to include a -. Hence, `address` is an invalid component and `person-address` is a valid one.

A very common requirement of web applications is to include a copyright footer. Let's create a component to include the company's copyright footer in their application:

1. The first thing to do is to create a new file in `app/templates/components` directory called as `copyright-footer.hbs`, with the following contents:

```
<footer>
  <div>
    © 20014-2015 Ember.js Essentials by Packt Publishing
  </div>
  <div>
    Content is available under MIT license
  </div>
</footer>
```

   The copyright-footer.hbs is present at chapter7/example1/app/templates/components/copyright-footer.hbs

2. To use the above component, we can now include the `{{copyright-footer}}` in our templates and that would render the copyright footer there.

3. Let's add the component in our `application.hbs` file, present at `app/templates/`:

```
<h2 id='title'>Welcome to Ember.js</h2>

{{outlet}}
{{copyright-footer}}
```

The application.hbs is present at chapter7/example1/app/templates/application.hbs

This will result in the copyright footer being present in all the pages of our application.

Passing data to your component

Till now, we saw the case wherein there was static data in our component templates, but to make components reusable, it often requires that some data of the component be made configurable and is passed in to it. This is also one of the main advantages of using components: if you pass in the correct configuration of the components, it works correctly no matter which place the component is included in.

Let's create a new component called as `product-description`, which displays the product data passed into it:

1. For that, let's create a file named `product-description.hbs` at `app/templates/components/` directory. This template file will contain the components of the product description. Since the data for product specification template changes with the product, this data should be passed in while using the component.

2. When building this template, we can assume that this data will be passed in explicitly, and will be accessible using standard handlebars syntax.

```
<h4>
  <span> {{name}} </span>
</h4>
<div>
  <table>
    <tr>
      <td> M.R.P </td>
      <td> {{MRP}}</td>
    </tr>
    <tr>
```

```
      <td> Price </td>
      <td> {{price}}</td>
    </tr>
    <tr>
      <td> You Save </td>
      <td> {{sale}} </td>
    </tr>
  </table>
</div>
```

The product description component is present at
chapter7/example1/app/templates/components/product-description.hbs

As you can see, we have made name, MRP, price, and sale of a product configurable, and should be passed in explicitly when using the component.

3. Now in order to pass in the data to a component, we can simply do like the following code snippet:

```
{{product-description name="Product Name"  MRP="$ 100"
  price="$80" sale="$20"}}
```

You could also fetch the MRP, price, and sale property from your route's model object as follows:

```
{{#product-description name="Product Name"  MRP=model.MRP
  price=model.price sale=model.sale}}
```

The model can return the appropriate object by either fetching it from the server, or returning a static object as follows:

```
import Ember from 'ember';

export default Ember.Route.extend({
  model: function(){
    return { MRP:"$ 100",price:"$80",sale:"$20"};
  }
});
```

The index route returning a static model object is present at chapter7/example1/app/routes/index.js

4. If you run the example and visit `http://localhost:4200/` on your machine, you will see something like the following:

Welcome to Ember.js

Product Name

M.R.P $ 100
Price $80
You Save $20

© 20014-2015 Ember.js Essentials by Packt Publishing
Content is available under MIT license

The Index page for example1 including product description and copyright-footer components

Providing custom HTML to your components

We started rendering components with static HTML content, and then moved on to passing the data to our components. Now, what if we want to use our components as layouts, and provide them the HTML content that should be rendered within the component at a designated place?

Let's make it more clear with an example. We will continue with the previous example, in which we passed in the data for product description to our component. Till now, we have been showing the product MRP, price, and sale values, but now we want to add the product information. The problem with product information is that the information format might change, based on the type of product we are using. Our component should be flexible enough to accommodate different product information formats.

Components also have the ability to be used in block forms. Block form is very similar to handlebars {{#if}}. We discussed blocks in *Chapter 3, Rendering Using Templates*. The block form of a component starts with {{#component-name}}, and ends with {{/component-name}}.

In order for components to be usable in block form, we have defined the components in such a way that they capture the data that is present inside the component block. Ember.js framework lets you do that with the yield Handlebars.js helper method.

Let's see how we can use the yield helper to capture the product information of any product:

```
<h4>
    <span> {{name}} </span>
</h4>
<div>
  <table>
    <tr>
      <td> M.R.P </td>
      <td> {{MRP}}</td>
    </tr>
    <tr>
      <td> Price </td>
      <td> {{price}}</td>
    </tr>
    <tr>
      <td> You Save </td>
      <td> {{sale}} </td>
    </tr>
  </table>
  <div class="information">
    {{yield}}
  </div>
</div>
```

The product description component is present at
chapter7/example1/app/templates/components/product-description.hbs

As you may have noticed, we have added an additional block to contain the product information. This div is assigned a class, information, which controls the UI properties of the information block, and has a {{yield}} helper inside it. This yield helper method tells the component that the content will be provided by the template that is using this component. The yield helper will capture the content that is present inside the component tag when it is used in block form.

Now we can use the {{product-description}} component in our template in block form and provide in the HTML for product information within it, as follows:

```
{{#product-description name="Product Name"  MRP="$ 100"
  price="$80" sale="$20"}}
  <ul>
    <li> Info 1</li>
    <li> Info 2</li>
    <li> Info 3</li>
    <li> Info 4</li>
  </ul>
{{/product-description}}
```

The index template using the product description component

This will result in product page, which looks like this:

Welcome to Ember.js

Product Name

M.R.P $ 100
Price $80
You Save $20

- Info 1
- Info 2
- Info 3
- Info 4

© 20014-2015 Ember.js Essentials by Packt Publishing
Content is available under MIT license

The Index template providing HTML content to the product description component

Extending Ember.Component

Till now, we have been using Ember components in their default form. Ember.js lets you programmatically customize the component you are building by backing them with your own component JavaScript class.

Changing your component's tag

One of the most common use case for backing your component with custom JavaScript code is to wrap your component in a tag, other than the default `<div>` tag.

When you include a component in your template, the component is by default rendered inside a div tag. For instance, we included the copyright footer component in our application template using `{{copyright-footer}}`. This resulted in the following HTML code:

```
<div id="ember391" class="ember-view">
<footer>
    <div>
        © 20014-2015 Ember.js Essentials by Packt Publishing
    </div>
    <div>
        Content is available under MIT license
    </div>
</footer>
</div>
```

The copyright footer component HTML enclosed within a <div> tag

You can see that the copyright component's content is enclosed inside a div that has an ID `ember391` and class `ember-view`. This works for most of the cases, but sometimes you may want to change this behavior to enclose the component in the enclosing tag of your choice. To do that, let's back our component with a matching component JavaScript class.

Let's take an instance in which we need to wrap the text in a `<p>` tag, rather than a `<div>` tag for the about us page of our application.

All the components of the JavaScript classes go inside the `app/components` folder. The file name of the JavaScript component class should be the same as the file name of the component's template that goes inside the `app/templates/components/` folder.

For the above use case, first let's create a component JavaScript class, whose contents should be wrapped inside a `<p>` tag. Let us create a new file inside the `app/components` folder named `about-us-intro.js`, with the following contents:

```
import Ember from 'ember';

export default Ember.Component.extend({
  tagName: "p"
});
```

The about-us component JavaScript class is present at chapter-7/example1/app/components/about-us-intro.js

As you can see, we extended the `Ember.Component` class and overrode the `tagName` property to use a `p` tag instead of the `div` tag.

Now, let us create the template for this component. The Ember.js framework will look for the matching template for the above component at `app/templates/components/about-us-intro.hbs`.

As we are enclosing the contents of the `about-us-intro` component in the `<p>` tag, we can simply write the `about us` introduction in the template as follows:

```
This is the about us introduction.Everything that is present here
  will be enclosed within a &lt;p&gt; tag.
```

The contents of chapter-7/example1/app/components/about-us-intro.hbs

We can now include the `{{about-us-intro}}` in our templates, and it will wrap the above text inside the `<p>` tag.

Now, if you visit the `http://localhost:4200/about-us` page, you should see the preceding text wrapped inside the `<p>` tag.

In the preceding example, we used a fixed `tagName` property in our component's class. But, in reality, the `tagName` property of our component could be a computed property in your controller or model class that uses your own custom logic to derive the `tagName` of the component:

```
import Ember from "ember";
export default Ember.ObjectController.extend({
  tagName: function(){
    //do some computation logic here
    return "p";
  }.property()
});
```

The about-us controller is present at chapter-7/example1/app/controllers/about-us.js

Then, you can override the default `tagName` property, with your own computed `tagName` from the controller:

```
{{about-us-intro tagName=tagName}}
```

For very simple cases, you don't even need to define your custom component's JavaScript class. You can override the properties such as `tagName` and others of your component when you use the component tag:

```
{{about-us-intro tagName="p"}}
```

Here, since you did not create a custom component class, the Ember.js framework generates one for you in the background, and then overrides the `tagName` property to use `p`, instead of `div`.

Adding custom CSS classes to your component

Similar to the `tagName` property of your component, you can also add additional CSS classes and customize the attributes of your HTML tags by using custom component classes.

To provide static class names that should be applied to your components, you can override the `classNames` property of your component. The `classNames` property if of type array should be assigned properties accordingly. Let's continue with the above example, and add two additional classes to our component:

```
import Ember from 'ember';

export default Ember.Component.extend({
    tagName: "p",
    classNames: ["intro","text"]
});
```

This will add two additional classes, `intro` and `text`, to the generated `<p>` tag.

If you want to bind your class names to other component properties, you can use the `classNameBinding` property of the component as follows:

```
export default Ember.Component.extend({
  tagName: "p",
  classNameBindings: ["intro","text"],
  intro: "intro-css-class",
  text: "text-css-class"
});
```

This will produce the following HTML for your component:

```
<p id="ember401" class="ember-view intro-css-class
   text-css-class">This is the about us introduction.Everything
   that is present here will be enclosed within a &lt;p&gt;
   tag.</p>
```

As you can see, the `<p>` tag now has additional `intro-css-class` and `text-css-class` classes added. The `classNameBindings` property of the component tells the framework to bind the class attribute of the HTML tag of the component with the provided properties of the component.

In case the property provided inside the `classNameBindings` returns a boolean value, the class names are computed differently. If the bound property returns a `true` boolean value, then the name of the property is used as the class name and is applied to the component. On the other hand, if the bound property returns to `false`, then no class is applied to the component.

Let us see this in an example:

```
import Ember from 'ember';

export default Ember.Component.extend({
  tagName: "p",
  classNames: ["static-class","another-static-class"],
  classNameBindings: ["intro","text","trueClass","falseClass"],
  intro: "intro-css-class",
  text: "text-css-class",
  trueClass: function(){
    //Do Some logic
    return true;
  }.property(),
  falseClass: false
});
```

The about-us-intro component is present at chapter-7/example1/app/components/about-us-intro.js

Continuing with the above `about-us-intro` component, you can see that we have added two additional strings in the `classNameBindings` array, namely, `trueClass` and `falseClass`. Now, when the framework tries to bind the `trueClass` to the corresponding component's property, it sees that the property is returning a boolean value and not a string, and then computes the class names accordingly.

The above component shall produce the following HTML content:

```
<p id="ember401" class="ember-view static-class
  another-static-class intro-css-class text-css-class true-class">
  This is the about us introduction.Everything that is present
  here will be enclosed within a &lt;p&gt; tag.
</p>
```

Notice that in the given example, `true-class` was added instead of `trueClass`. The Ember.js framework is intelligent enough to understand the conventions used in CSS class names, and automatically converts our `trueClass` to a valid `true-class`.

Adding custom attributes to your component's DOM element

Till now, we have seen how we can change the default tag and CSS classes for your component. Ember.js frameworks let you specify and customize HTML attributes for your component's **DOM** (**Document Object Model**) element.

Many JavaScript libraries also use HTML attributes to provide additional details about the DOM element.

Ember.js framework provides us with `attributeBindings` to bind different HTML attributes with component's properties. The `attributeBindings` which is similar to `classNameBindings`, is also of array type and works very similarly to it.

Let's create a new component, called as `{{ember-image}}`, by creating a file at `app/component/ember-image.js`, and use attributes bindings to bind the `src`, `width`, and `height` attributes of the `<img>` tag.

```
import Ember from 'ember';

export default Ember.Component.extend({
  tagName: "img",
  attributeBindings: ["src","height","width"],
  src: "http://emberjs.com/images/logos/ember-logo.png",
  height:"80px",
  width:"200px"
});
```

The ember-image component is present at chapter7/example1/app/components/ember-image.js

This will result in the following HTML:

```
<img
  id="ember401"
  class="ember-view"
  src="http://emberjs.com/images/logos/ember-logo.png"
  height="80px"
  width="200px">
```

There could be cases in which you would want to use a different component's property name and a different HTML attribute name. For those cases, you can use the following notation:

```
attributeBindings: ["componentProperty:HTML-DOM-property]
import Ember from 'ember';

export default Ember.Component.extend({
  tagName: "img",
  attributeBindings: ["componentProperty:HTML-DOM-property],
  componentProperty: "value"
});
```

This will result in the the following HTML code:

```
<img id="ember402" HTML-DOM-property="value">
```

Handling actions for your component

Now that we have learned to create and customize Ember.js components, let's see how we can make our components interactive and handle different user interactions with our component.

Components are unique in the way they handle user interactions or the action events that are defined in the templates. The way we trigger actions from Ember.js components is identical to what we discussed in *Chapter 3, Rendering Using Templates* using the same {{action}} Handlebars.js helper method. The only difference is that the events from a component's template are sent directly to the component, and they don't bubble up to controllers or routes. If the event that is emitted from a component's template is not handled in Ember.Component instance, then that event will be ignored and will do nothing.

Let's create a component that has a lot of text inside it, but the full text is only visible if you click on the **Show More** button:

For that, we will have to first create the component's template. So let us create a new file, `long-text.hbs`, in the `app/templates/components/` folder. The contents of the template should have a **Show More** and **Show Less** button, which show the full text and hide the additional text, respectively.

```
<p>
   This is a long text and we intend to show only this much unless
   the user presses the show more button below.
</p>
{{#if showMoreText}}
   This is the remaining text that should be visible when we press
   the show more button. Ideally this should contain a lot more
   text, but for example's sake this should be enough.
   <br>
   <br>
   <button {{action "toggleMore"}}> Show Less </button>
{{else}}
   <button {{action "toggleMore"}}> Show More </button>
{{/if}}
```

The long-text component is present at chapter-7/example1/app/templates/components/long-text.hbs

As you can see, we use the `{{action}}` helper method in our component's template to trigger actions on the component.

In order for the above template to work properly, we need to handle the `toggleMore` in our component class. So, let's create `long-text.js` at `app/components/` folder.

```
import Ember from 'ember';

export default Ember.Component.extend({
   showMoreText: false,
   actions:{
    toggleMore: function(){
        this.toggleProperty("showMoreText");
    }
   }
});
```

The long-text.js is present at chapter-7/example1/app/components/long-text.js

All action handlers should go inside the actions object, which is present in the component definition. As you can see, we have added a `toggleMore` action handler inside the actions object in the component's definition. The `toggleMore` just toggles the boolean property `showMoreText` that we use in the template to show or hide text.

When the above component is included in `about-us` template, it should present a brief text, followed by the **Show More** button. When you click the **Show More** button, the rest of text appears and the **Show Less** button appears, which, when clicked on, should hide the text.

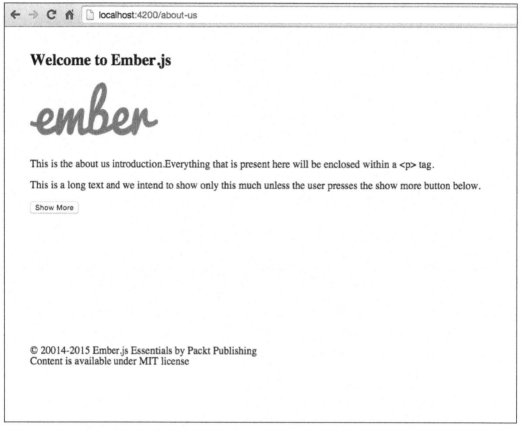

The long-text component being used at the about-us page showing only limited text, followed by the Show More button

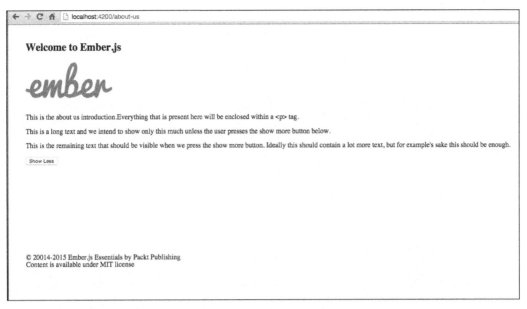

Clicking Show More shows more text on the screen along with the Show Less button to rollback

Mapping component actions to the rest of your application

Till now, we have been successful in creating self-contained reusable components. These components render themselves and handle actions that can be served in isolation, irrespective of where the components are being used.

As we learned earlier in the chapter, events that are raised from the component's template are looked up in the component's action object. These events don't bubble up to the application's controllers or routes.

This all works fine till the components need to inform the rest of the application to take some business decisions. Ember.js framework lets your components translate the component events into meaningful application actions by using the `sendAction` method, accessible by the component.

Let's see that by an example. Let us create a `date-picker` component that is reusable across our application. But we would also want to invoke the context application specific method that is invoked when the user focuses out of the date picker.

Let's create the date picker template `date-picker.hbs` in the `app/templates/components/` directory. This template will be a simple one with only the following contents:

```
<input type="date" name="date" {{action "submit" on="focusOut"}}>
```

The date-picker template is present at chapter-7/example1/app/templates/components/date-picker.hbs

As you can see, it's a simple input field of type `date`, and triggers the `submit` event on the component, when the user focuses out of the `date-picker`.

Now, let's use this component inside our index template:

```
<div>Please set the product's manufactoring date : {{date-picker
  action="saveMaufactoringDate"}}</div>
<br>
<div>Please set the product's expiry date : {{date-picker
  action="saveExpiryDate"}}</div>
<br>
<div>The Manufactoring Date Set By You is
  {{manufactoringDate}}</div>
<div>The Expiry Date Set By You is {{expiryDate}}</div>
```

Date-picker component being used in index template is present at chapter7/example1/app/templates/index.hbs

As you can see, we are using the same component at multiple places; the only difference is that we pass in different action names each time we use the component. This action tells the component the name of the controller or route action that should be manually triggered when the component is used. In order for the component to send the action to respective controller or route, we need to define the behavior in our component class. So, let's create `date-picker.js` in `app/components/` directory:

```
import Ember from 'ember';

export default Ember.Component.extend({
  actions:{
    submit: function(){
      var date = this.$("input").val();
      this.sendAction('action',date);
    }
  }
});
```

The content of date-picker.js component is present at chapter-7/example1/app/components/ directory

As you can see, that component has a submit action defined inside the actions object; the submit action is triggered when the user focuses out of the `date-picker`. Inside the submit action we get the value of the input box, and call the `sendAction` method:

```
var date = this.$("input").val();
this.sendAction('action',date);
```

In the `sendAction` method, we pass in the name of the property that provides the name of the action that should be called on the controller or route, followed by the argument that should be supplied to the action, as follows:

```
{{date-picker action="saveMaufactoringDate"}}
```

So, in the preceding case, when we call `this.sendAction('action',date)`, the `saveMaufactoringDate` event is looked up first in the respective controller and then in the route hierarchy.

So, in order to save the manufacturing date, we will have to handle the `saveMaufactoringDate` action in the index controller actions object. Till now, we were using the default controller that is auto-generated by the framework, but now, as we need to handle the action in the controller, we will have to define it in our application.

Let's create index.js in `app/controller/` directory to define our controller. The index controller should handle both of `saveMaufactoringDate` and `saveExpiryDate`:

```
import Ember from "ember";
export default Ember.ObjectController.extend({
  manufactoringDate: "",
  expiryDate:"",
  actions: {
    saveMaufactoringDate: function(date){
      this.set("manufactoringDate",date);
    },
    saveExpiryDate: function(date){
      this.set("expiryDate",date);
    }
  }
});
```

The index controller is present at chapter-7/example1/app/controllers/index.js

So now, when we select the date in the date-picker, the respective property will be set on the controller. If you run the `example1` application under `chapter-7`, and then navigate to `http://localhost:4200/`, you will see the following contents:

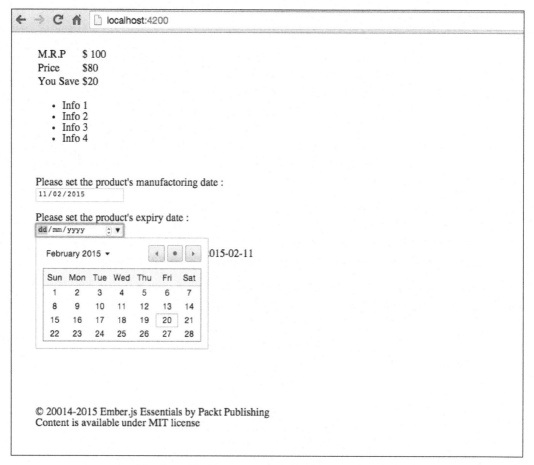

The date-picker component in use in the index template

Now that we have used the `sendAction` method to notify the controller about the action from the component, let's discuss some other variations of the `sendAction` method.

When we used the `sendAction` method from our `app/components/date-picker.js`, we used `this.sendAction('action',date)`. This would bubble up the event `saveManufactoringDate` or `saveExpiryDate` with the method argument, as `date` to the application. This is the same event that we assigned to the action property when using the component in our templates:

```
{{date-picker action="saveMaufactoringDate"}}
{{date-picker action="saveExpiryDate"}}
```

If we don't have arguments to be bubbled up to the controller or the route hierarchy, then we can also call `this.sendAction()`. Calling `this.sendAction()` would automatically extract the event name from the action property of the component, and bubble up the event to the respective controller or route hierarchy.

On the other hand, if we want to send multiple events to our controllers based on some action on the component, we can define the events while using the components as follows:

```
{{date-picker action1="someControllerAction1" action2="
  someControllerAction2"}}
```

And then, we can use `this.sendAction('action1',date)` and `this.sendAction('action2',date)` from our component.

Summary

In this chapter, we learned about how we can build custom reusable components in Ember.js. We started with the introduction of Ember views and components, and learned that Ember.js framework is focusing more on Ember components rather than Ember views going forward. Then, we learned how easy it is to define your own components and use them in your templates. We then delved into the detail of Ember components, and learned how we can pass in data from our template's context to our component. This was followed by how can we programmatically extend the `Ember.Component` class, and customize our component's attributes, including the tag type, HTML attributes, and CSS classes. Finally, we learned how we send the component's actions to respective controllers, and route hierarchy using the `sendAction` method.

Index

A

action
event bubbling 55-60
handling, for components 142, 143
adapter 113
AJAX (asynchronous JavaScript and XML) 3
ambitious web applications 2, 3
AMD (asynchronous module definition)
URL 7
application
component actions, mapping to 145-149
state 67, 68
array controller 92-96
array helper methods
URL 38
asset pipeline 6, 7

B

bindings
across objects 36, 37
bower
URL 9, 10
broccoli
assets 6
URL 6

C

coding by convention 3
component actions
mapping, to application 145-149

components
about 130
actions, handling for 142, 143
custom attributes, adding to
DOM element 141, 142
custom CSS classes, adding to 139, 140
custom HTML, providing to 134-136
data, passing to 132, 133
defining 131
tag, modifying of 137-139
computed properties
about 29
getter methods 29-34
setter methods 29-34
conditionals, Handlebars.js
about 47
else 48, 49
if 48, 49
unless 48, 49
controllers
about 89
array controller 91-96
connecting 96-98
object controller 91-96
setting up 82, 83
use cases 89-91
convention over configuration 3
CORS (cross-origin resource sharing) 119
custom attributes
adding, to component's
DOM element 141, 142

URL 19

H

Handlebars 42, 43
Handlebars.js
  conditionals 47
  expressions 45-47
  helpers 62-65
  input helpers 61, 62
  used, for displaying items list 50-52
  used, for JavaScript templates 39-41
handlebar templates 5
HTMLBars 42, 43
HTML tag attributes
  binding 52-55

I

identity map 108

J

JavaScript 3
JavaScript templates
  Handlebars.js used 39-41
JSON (JavaScript Object Notation) 114

L

location API 87

M

many to many relationship 106, 107
mixin 27, 28
model
  injecting, for templates 76-79
Model View Controller (MVC pattern)
  about 4
  Controller 5
  Model 5
  Router/Route 5
  Templates 5
  View/Component 5

N

nested templates 72-76
node
  URL 10
node package manager
  URL 9

O

object controller 91-96
objects
  bindings 36, 37
observers 34, 35
one to many relationship 105, 106
one to one relationship 104, 105

P

PhantomJS
  URL 10
prototype extensions 37, 38

R

records
  finding 112
  modifying 113
  working with 109-111
RequireJS
  URL 7
resources 72-76
REST adapter 113-116
REST (Representational State Transfer) 114
router 68
routes
  controller, setting up 82, 83
  creating 68-71
  making dynamic 79-81
  serialize method 82

modules 7
mustache templates
  URL 42

S

SEO (search engine optimization) 70
separation of concerns (SoC) 47
sideloaded relationships 116, 117
Single Responsibility Principle 107
store 107
String helper
   URL 38

T

tag
   modifying, of components 137-139

templates
customizing, to render 83-86
defining 43-45
model, injecting 76-79

U

URL endpoints
   customizing 118, 119

W

web component 131

Thank you for buying
Ember.js Web Development
with Ember CLI

About Packt Publishing

Packt, pronounced 'packed', published its first book, *Mastering phpMyAdmin for Effective MySQL Management*, in April 2004, and subsequently continued to specialize in publishing highly focused books on specific technologies and solutions.

Our books and publications share the experiences of your fellow IT professionals in adapting and customizing today's systems, applications, and frameworks. Our solution-based books give you the knowledge and power to customize the software and technologies you're using to get the job done. Packt books are more specific and less general than the IT books you have seen in the past. Our unique business model allows us to bring you more focused information, giving you more of what you need to know, and less of what you don't.

Packt is a modern yet unique publishing company that focuses on producing quality, cutting-edge books for communities of developers, administrators, and newbies alike. For more information, please visit our website at www.packtpub.com.

About Packt Open Source

In 2010, Packt launched two new brands, Packt Open Source and Packt Enterprise, in order to continue its focus on specialization. This book is part of the Packt Open Source brand, home to books published on software built around open source licenses, and offering information to anybody from advanced developers to budding web designers. The Open Source brand also runs Packt's Open Source Royalty Scheme, by which Packt gives a royalty to each open source project about whose software a book is sold.

Writing for Packt

We welcome all inquiries from people who are interested in authoring. Book proposals should be sent to author@packtpub.com. If your book idea is still at an early stage and you would like to discuss it first before writing a formal book proposal, then please contact us; one of our commissioning editors will get in touch with you.

We're not just looking for published authors; if you have strong technical skills but no writing experience, our experienced editors can help you develop a writing career, or simply get some additional reward for your expertise.

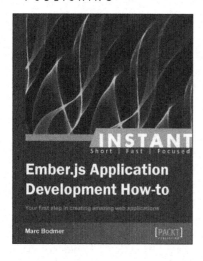

Instant Ember.js Application Development How-to

ISBN: 978-1-78216-338-1   Paperback: 48 pages

Your first step in creating amazing web applications

1. Learn something new in an Instant!
   A short, fast, focused guide delivering
   immediate results.

2. Create semantic HTML templates
   using Handlebars.

3. Lay the foundation for large web applications
   using the latest version of Ember.js in an easy
   to follow format.

4. Follow clear and concise examples to build up a
   fully working application.

Mastering Ember.js

ISBN: 978-1-78398-198-4   Paperback: 218 pages

Build fast, scalable, dynamic, and ambitious
single-page web applications by mastering Ember.js

1. Create, test, and deploy powerful and
   professional web applications.

2. Debug and modularize your project effectively.

3. Easily architect solutions to any single page
   web application needs.

open source
community experience distilled

[PACKT]
PUBLISHING

Rapid Ember.js
William Hart

Rapid Ember.js [Video]

ISBN: 978-1-78439-765-4   Duration: 01:00 hour

Build dynamic and data-driven web applications from the ground up using Ember.js

1. Build nested and detailed application structures easily with Ember's router.

2. Enrich your web applications with Ember's powerful data-bound features.

3. Update your web page content and styles based on the underlying data automatically.

Learning Single-page
Web Application Development

Build powerful and scalable single-page web applications using a full stack JavaScript environment with Node.js, MongoDB, AngularJS, and the Express framework

Fernando Monteiro

Learning Single-page Web Application Development

ISBN: 978-1-78355-209-2   Paperback: 214 pages

Build powerful and scalable single-page web applications using a full stack JavaScript environment with Node.js, MongoDB, AngularJS, and the Express framework

1. Deal with user authentication on single page web application.

2. Test with Karma and Protractor.

3. Continuous deployment with automated tools.

Please check **www.PacktPub.com** for information on our titles

CPSIA information can be obtained
at www.ICGtesting.com
Printed in the USA
FSOW03n0920090615
7758FS